Real-Time Proven Commodity Spreads

REAL-TIME PROVEN COMMODITY SPREADS

The 20 Most Consistently Profitable Low-Risk Trades

By George Angell

Windsor Books, Brightwaters, N.Y.

Published by Windsor Books
P. O. Box 280
Brightwaters, N.Y., 11718

Manufactured in the United States of America

ISBN 0-930233-02-6

For Robert, Gail and Susan

Acknowledgements

For providing me with invaluable assistance, without which this book could not have been written, I'd like to express my gratitude to Michael Marriott, president of MJK Associates in Santa Clara, California. MJK's computerized data bank really made the book possible. For without access to the data bank and the necessary programs available from MJK to retrieve the kind of specialized information called for in my research, this endeavor could have taken many, many years to accomplish. I highly recommend MJK to anyone seeking to test a trading system or simply interested in obtaining clean commodity futures data.

George Angell

Table of Contents

Figures

Tables

Preface

When the first edition of this book appeared in the fall of 1980 inflation was still raging. The metals and grain markets were still booming, although they were about to enter sustained bear markets; stock index futures were still unheard of among futures traders, the Treasury bill market was active; options on futures contracts didn't exist; and tax spreads were still accepted by the IRS. So much has changed since then. In five short years, financial futures, although no doubt still in their infancy, are surging ahead in volume and popularity while the agricultural markets, together with the farmers, are on the ropes. Markets have come and gone since then. Does anyone remember that the Chicago Board of Trade had a CD contract? Or the Chicago Merc's flirtation with gasoline futures? Other markets have simply disappeared. Remember plywood? Gone the way of broilers and eggs. Today, there is a greater institutional participation in the markets than ever before. Corporations trying to hedge against foreign currency risks; banks trying to out-guess the Fed's next pronouncement; that sort of thing. Perhaps the most important significant change in the markets has been the attitude toward tomorrow—namely, inflation. Once an ever-constant preoccupation, inflation worriers are on the decline—a sign, no doubt, that a new spat of inflation is right around the corner!

Fortunately, despite the roller-coaster ride the economy has taken in recent years, interest in the futures market is still strong. Traders are still interested in spreads, especially the seasonal ones which can be counted upon to work through good times and bad. Spreads, in short, which are reliable.

I must confess that I approached doing this second edition of the book with a certain amount of trepidation. What if the computer printout revealed that the spreads I originally pinpointed as reliable seasonal plays proved losers? What if the very notion of seasonality proved inherently misguided? What if the numbers just didn't work? Perhaps surprisingly, my fears were unfounded. For one, I'd been following some of the spreads on an informal basis for two or three years. And they looked just fine. Take the pork belly spread. When I'd last counted, it had been working consistently for ten or eleven years. That's money in the bank, year after year. What the computer showed was that it has a 100 percent track record. It has made money every year since 1972, 13 years in all. If you want consistency, you can't beat that. But if you are looking for an increase in profitablilty, as opposed to simple consistency, you have to consider the live hogs spread. Net profits increased by 90 percent in the past five years; the spread has averaged almost $1,000 a year—all on a $500 margin investment.

A real concern, I must admit, was the soybeans and the grains in general. After all, the beans offered the big opportunities in spread trading, with substantial volatility sometimes approaching $10,000 in a single spread. Given the bearish sentiment in all farm commodities in recent years, the results are somewhat predictable. The normal-seasonal strategies—namely, the bull spreads—have been a disaster. But the contra-seasonal strategies have worked pretty consistently. In just five years and three trades, the contra-seasonal long November-short July soybean spread earned almost $13,000 in profits. While the meal and oil spreads have offered nothing to write home about in the last five years, the corn, wheat, and oats spreads all made money.

But perhaps the most remarkable insight of the new statistics which are published here for the first time are that the *bear spreads work most consistently*. Sell a front month and buy a back month. Could it be that this strategy, among the hundreds of techniques utilized by futures traders in bull and bear markets alike, is the most consistently reliable one? After all, this was an insight from my first study of seasonal spreads. Regardless of when spreads "widen," they seem to "narrow" on a much more consistent basis. What's more, when they get "out of line"—say, July beans 35¢ or more over November in the fall—it is time to sell the store, the pattern becomes so reliable. My one concern in advocating the back spreads is that every four years or so the bean market starts to skyrocket—and it's almost time for another flight. So caution is advised.

As for the losers, nobody's perfect. Our sugar spread took a nose dive along with cocoa and cotton. True, these markets are in the doldrums. But no one stays down forever, and chances are these spreads will begin to work again. What's important is that we've now assembled greater evidence that certain spreads offer a higher probability of proving profitable than others. By carefully selecting those computer-proven spreads and patiently allowing them to work in your favor through the power of seasonality, you put yourself in a position to win in this competitive game. The purpose of this book is to make you successful with spreads. Happy trading.

How To Use This Book

This book is designed to serve two primary audiences—those who may be new to spread trading and require a complete introduction to the field, and those who may already be adept at spreading, but require a somewhat more specialized look at specific spread relationships. Both can use the book with profit.

If you are new to spread trading, I strongly suggest you read Chapter One first. Since I have a somewhat unique method of talking about spread relationships, more experienced traders might find the material contained in Chapter One useful as well.

The book is intended primarily as a reference and trading guide. Each major commodity group has its own section, and a complete chapter is devoted to the major seasonal commodities. Hopefully, at a glance, you will be able to tell what a given spread has done over the past several years. While not always useful, this information does have a cumulative value in that seasonal growing and harvest periods tend to cause certain contracts to be strong or weak. Whenever possible, I've tried to provide an indication of just how successful any given spread has been in the past. When no clearcut pattern exists in the spread, I've often included it anyway in the interest of being comprehensive.

Please be aware that seasonal patterns sometimes occur in spreads that aren't influenced by growing seasons—financial futures being a ready example—and, whenever possible, I've included these "nonseasonal" seasonals as well. Because the nature of the markets has changed so much since the early 1970's, I did not think it prudent to research spreads before that period. A glance at any historical price chart will show that virtually every commodity futures contract now trading has truly "come alive" in price action at some time during the seventies. Moreover, financial futures and other new contracts have only begun to exert their influence in the marketplace. Looking ahead, the eighties will most certainly be a period of unprecedented growth in the futures industry. And the informed speculator will be best equipped to successfully trade the volatile markets to come.

While spreads are noted for their low-risk aspect, not all spreads offer low-risk; in fact, a few are quite risky—an observation that a number of speculators have learned to their ultimate chagrin. Nevertheless, I think spreads offer the best opportunity to earn consistent profits over time. This book is designed to identify those consistent winners. In a *Wall Street Journal* story published not long ago, one spread expert was quoted as saying that trading some spreads was like watching paint dry—not so exciting, but very predictable. Our interest here is to identify and analyze those spreads that offer the best opportunities to work like clockwork year after year.

This would-be spread trader must be cautioned that return is always commensurate with risk. The "sure-thing" trades are going to return comparatively small profits and the high-risk trades are going to return high profits. Moreover, one must always be prepared for the unexpected. Time after time, a bull spread will work well in a market that is overwhelmingly bearish—and vice versa. And even the consistent markets will occasionally move contra-cyclically. Typically, the contra-cyclical spread move will occur when you least expect it, throwing your analysis into disarray. To cope successfully with the unexpected, never fight the market. Just take a small loss and await the time when the spread is ready to work. Sooner or later, the fundamentals will prevail and the spread will move in the direction of the true underlying supply and demand situation.

Lastly, to make the most of this book, treat the information contained within as a departure point, and not the final word on spread trading. There are many, many spreads not covered in these pages and you may wish to launch your own investigation of potentially profitable trading opportunities. Certainly, there will be more and more as the futures explosion continues. Should you wish to research the history of spreads on your own, I recommend the computerized services of MJK Associates, 122 Saratoga Avenue, Santa Clara, California.

Introduction

When it comes to high-risk, high-gain speculation, nothing compares with commodity futures trading. Other investments may offer more safety, but they don't have the profit potential of commodities trading. And those that offer the kind of profit potential you will find in the futures market are apt to be illegal. Like most investors, I've tried making money a number of ways: stocks, bonds, options, bullion, mutual funds—you name it. Nothing compares with commodities. Not if you are interested in turning a comparatively small amount of money into a significant amount in a short period of time. But for most people, commodities trading has one major drawback—it is too risky. Just mention the word commodities among friends these days and you are likely to find someone telling you how he took a flier in corn or cattle and ended up in the loser column. It happens. In fact, it happens so frequently that I only become suspicious when I hear that someone made a killing in the market—a far less common occurrence.

The risks that accompany commodity trading are what make futures speculation so attractive. The key to huge profits and losses that are to be made or lost in the commodities market is leverage. Simply put, leverage means you put down a little and you control a lot. On the one hand, this leverage can magnify your gains tremendously; on the other, it can wipe you out. The old cliche about leverage being a double-edged sword is true; you just don't want it turned against you.

Introduction

A GAME OF ODDS

Despite the risks, commodity futures trading remains a highly attractive game to play. It is fast-paced, exiciting, and, with a little luck, can be enormously rewarding. It's been said that speculation in commodity futures has produced more millionaires under 30 than any profession with the exception of the rock music business. Yet it is a highly specialized undertaking—one that requires rigorous discipline and a keen mind. Above all, successful speculation requires an adroit manipulation of the odds. The winning commodity trader must routinely keep his risk level low if he is to exit the market with profits.

One technique that has won wide acceptance among professional traders is spread trading. Spread trading limits risk. it does so by playing both sides of the market at the same time. A spread involves having both a "long" or bought position and a "short" or sold position. The spreader profits not from an absolute change in the level of prices, but from a change of the "differential" between where a spread is initiated and where it is subsequently liquidated. There are numerous advantages to this approach to the market, which will be spelled out in the pages that follow. But a primary advantage is that it severely limits the prospect of sudden losses due to limit moves. When such sudden unexpected price movements do occur, their impact is minimized because the loss on one side, or "leg," of the spread is compensated for by a corresponding gain on the other side of the spread. It makes spread trading the ideal low-risk way to play the exciting futures game—and the ideal way to win consistent profits.

DIVERSE STRATEGIES

Spreads, like outright net position trades in which you either buy or sell a commodity, lend themselves to a number of market strategies. You can place spreads to benefit from seasonal price moves or use them to exploit rising or falling markets. Spreads work between different futures contracts of the same commodity or between different (but related) commodities, such as cattle and hogs, or soybeans and soybean oil. You can even place spreads in commodities trading on different exchanges, such as wheat traded in Chicago and wheat traded in Kansas City or Minneapolis. And some spreads, due to the nature of carrying charges (which will be explained fully), are absolutely limited in risk (a rarity in the futures markets) while capable of returning handsome profits.

Many professional traders use spreads exclusively in their market activities because they *know* the kind of risks that futures trading entails. But the bulk of all futures traders refuse to use spreads for a variety of reasons. Some would prefer to take their chances on a higher return in outright position trading, one more commensurate with the greater risk involved; some simply don't understand how spreads work. The professionals don't mind keeping this little-known market strategy to themselves because they earn their profits from the majority who lose—and don't use spreads. The professionals know the odds and they know how important it is to keep their risks low.

THE ADVANTAGES OF SPREADS

There are a number of reasons why spread trading offers the best way to earn consistent profits in the volatile commodities markets. What follows is a brief rundown of the key advantages.

Trade On Fundamentals Only: The nature of spreads (holding both a long and short position at the same time) enables them to be relatively immune to so-called "technical" price changes that are apt to move a market limit up or down within a short period of time. When sudden volatility hits a market, the absolute price of a commodity may change quickly while the spread price will often remain the same. This is especially true when a market is buffeted by rumors that cause limit moves. Should a market suddenly move limit down, the "longs" or buyers of the commodity will have substantial losses. However, a spread trader in the same market will probably be unaffected by the move because the loss on his long position will be fully compensated by a corresponding gain on his short position. Thus spread trading helps lessen the impact of abrupt up and down "whipsaw" technical price movements.

Limited Risk: When you trade outright positions, your exposure is virtually unlimited. If you are short a commodity and the markets begin to lock limit against you day-after-day, five or six trading sessions may go by before enough sellers enter the market to buy back your position. By that time, you may have lost all your margin money plus a lot more. With a spread, since you are both long and short at the same time, this kind of an extreme move is unlikely to happen. While most spreads are lower in risk than outright positions, there is also a type of spread known as a "limited-risk" spread. When properly placed, this type of spread is the safest trade you can make in the commodity futures market, because the risk is clearly defined at the outset. The limited-risk spread has the additional appeal of having virtually unlimited potential for gain.

19

Introduction

Seasonality: Spreads are perhaps best known for their many seasonal characteristics. Due to harvest pressures and the trading of two different crops at the same time, the tendency for some contract months to rise or fall faster than other months often results in spreading opportunities. On a seasonal basis, there are spreads that work virtually like clockwork every year, with one month generally going to a decided premium or discount within a one-or two-month time frame. For traders who decide to play the seasonal odds, these spreads often represent money in the bank year after year.

High Profitability: Because the margins on spreads are frequently much lower than those of outright position trades (usually one-third to one-quarter the size), the profits on spreads as a percentage of margin are often higher than profits on outright positions. Given the wide swings in price that commodity futures have experienced in recent years, it is not surprising that more and more traders are turning to spreads. Spreads offer the low-risk way to trade commodity futures. In addition, because of reduced margins, the initial cost of getting into the market is much lower with a spread than it normally is when you trade outright positions.

In the pages that follow, we will discuss the spread trade with a special emphasis on the most popular spreads and how to use them for their maximum profitability.

Chapter 1

The Fundamentals Of Commodity Spread Trading

A commodity spread consists of two positions in the same or related commodities that are simultaneously placed and held—one long and one short.

Because you both buy and sell a futures contract when you initiate a spread, your exposure to an adverse movement in the price of the respective contracts is greatly diminished. Sudden and unexpected price movements in the underlying commodity will rarely result in spread losses. The reason for this is that contract months of the same related commodities tend to move in tandem—one contract gaining when the other gains, and vice-versa. For the trader who is spread—both long and short the same commodity—the rise in price of one contract month will result in profits on his long position while a similar rise in another month will result in losses on his short position. The net result is a tradeoff; a loss on one side of the spread will be offset by a corresponding profit on the other side. This would be a prescription for getting nowhere fast, if it weren't for the fact that futures contracts tend to rise or fall at *different rates*. Thus, a spread that results in a gain of, say, 12 cents on the long leg might only be offset by a loss of 8 cents on the short leg. The net profit would be the difference of the two months, or 4 cents.

PROFITING FROM A PRICE DIFFERENTIAL

The spread trader attempts to profit from a change in the price differential between two futures contracts. Because some commodities tend to maintain a fixed price differential between contract months for long periods of time, the spread trader looks for a situation in which the price difference will change, or move "out of line." Typically, this occurs when strong bullish or bearish forces are felt in a market, causing a temporary imbalance in supply and demand to move the near-term contracts to a sharp premium or discount to other months. On other occasions, a spread will already be judged "out of line" by the trader and he will place his position to take advantage of a temporary imbalance in futures prices. Should his judgment prove correct, the months will fall back into line and he will be rewarded with profits.

The overall direction of futures prices is not the prime consideration in spread trading. Although price direction is a component of the successful spread analysis, the prime consideration is the direction in the movement of the spread—will it narrow or widen? Futures prices can move up or down over a wide range without causing a movement in the spread. In fact, even a limit move, which typically will cause euphoria or despair in the hearts of futures traders, will not concern the spread trader—if both his months move the daily limit. This is because the spread trader is betting on a change in the price differential between months—not on a change in the absolute price level. And this makes all the difference.

Let's consider an example. It is January 1981 and the spread trader sees an interesting opportunity in the feeder cattle market, where futures for March delivery are selling for $80.40 per hundredweight, just 35 cents below futures for May delivery at $80.75 per hundredweight. He reasons that near-term tightness in supply will have its greatest impact on the nearer March contract, perhaps even sending the March contract to a higher price or premium over May. At present, trading 35 cents below May, the March is selling at a discount. Thus, he expects the market to *invert*—to have the nearer contracts selling at higher prices than more distant or far-out contracts. Here's what happens. He places the spread on January 15 at a negative 35 point difference (March at $80.40 − May at $80.75 = − $.35) and holds the spread until February 15. By February 1, feeder cattle prices have risen, affecting every contract month. But, significantly, the nearer March contract has risen faster than the more distant May contract. While March has risen a total of $1.70 per hundredweight to $82.10, the May contract has risen just $.75 per hundredwight to $81.50. Thus a $1.70 profit on the nearer "long" position is offset by a 75 cent loss on the "short" position for a net difference of 95 cents, the equivalent of $399 per spread.* The beginning difference of − 35 added to the closing spread difference of + 60 results in the total profit on the spread of 95 points. The respective buy and sell calculations exclusive of commissions are as follows:

---

*   Because feeder cattle is traded in units of 42,000 pounds, each one point move is worth $4.20. Thus a 95 point move is worth 95 times that amount, or $399.

DATE	ACTION TAKEN	
January 15	Bought one contract March feeder cattle at $80.40	Sold one contract May feeder cattle at $80.75
February 15	Sold one contract March feeder cattle at $82.10	Bought one contract May feeder cattle at $81.50
Result:	$1.70 gain on March feeder cattle	$.75 loss on May feeder cattle

$714 profit on March contract
−315 loss on May contract
$399 profit, exclusive of commissions

The typical response to an illustration such as this is: Why spread at all? If you know the price of feeder cattle is about to rise $1.70, why not simply buy March 1981 feeder cattle and participate in the full $1.70 move? It's a good question. Obviously, it would be more profitable to earn $1.70 in an outright net long position than just 95 cents in a spread. The answer has to do with probabilities. You never know for sure what the market is going to do. With a spread you have considerable protection that you don't have when you simply trade an outright position. For instance, if the feeder cattle market suddenly fell $5.00 per hundredweight when you held the long position, you would be out $2,100 plus commissions. But if the March contract fell five dollars when you were spread against May, chances are the May would likewise fall and recoup much of the loss on the long position. The rate at which the two contracts fell relative to one another would determine your profit or loss—if any.

Let's consider the impact of a sharp market decline when you are spread long March feeder cattle against short May feeder cattle. Since the nearby months tend to be more sensitive to the prevailing market sentiment for the cash commodity, the largest moves tend to occur in the nearbys. Thus, bearish news might cause March to decline by 70 cents while May falls by only 40 cents. This decline would result in a loss of 30 cents per spread, or the difference between what was lost on the nearby long and what was gained on the distant short. There is, of course, the possibility that the May would fall faster than the March, resulting in a profit on the spread. And a third possibility is that both months would fall or rise at the same rate, resulting in no change in the spread, neither a profit or loss.

23

The point: a spread trader profits from a change in the price differential—not from a change, either up or down, in the general level of prices.

HOW SMALL MARGINS
GENERATE DRAMATIC SPREAD PROFITS

Leverage, which is the key to enormous profitability of futures trading in general, plays an even more important role in spread trading. As a rule, the leverage in the typical futures trade ranges from about 20 to 1 (when the required margin is just 5 percent of the total value of the contract) to about 5 to 1 (when 20 percent margin of the total value of the contract is required). Compared to the stock market, where the best leverage you can get is 2 to 1 by buying on 50 percent margin, the leverage in commodity futures trading is very attractive indeed. But even when you are trading on 5 percent margin—that is, when your $5,000 in margin money controls a futures contract worth $100,000—you are giving up some of the magnifying power of leverage by not using spreads. Here's why. The margins on outright position trades are often as much as 10 times as high as the margin requirements on spreads of the comparable commodity. But on a relative basis, spreads are often much more than one-tenth as volatile as the outright position. Thus, dollar-for-dollar you get more profit-magnifying leverage when you trade spreads!

Let's take a hypothetical example in hogs. During a one month period in the fall of 1978, hog futures for delivery the following June rose more than six cents on the Chicago Mercantile Exchange. To gain this six cent profit, or $1,800, a trader need have only purchased June hogs and subsequently sold them a month later. At the time, the typical margin for an outright position was $2,000, give or take a few hundred dollars, depending on the brokerage house. On the $2,000 margin, the $1,800 profit represented a full 90 percent of invested monies—an impressive profit. But a spread trader might have done even better percentage-wise by purchasing June 1979 hogs and selling October 1979 hogs. Because spreads are inherently safer than outright position trades, the margin would be considerably less than $2,000, probably about one-fourth as much, or $500. Using the same $2,000 in equity, the spread trader might then have proceeded to place four June-October hog spreads. Compared to the move in the outright position, the spread's volatility was only about half as much, about 3½ cents as compared with 6 cents. Yet the smaller profit was generated on a smaller margin, resulting in a *larger percentage profit* in the spread. In all, the four June-October hog spreads generated a total profit of $4,200, while the single June hogs position returned just $1,800—less than half as much. The percentage profit in the spread was 210 percent, as compared to just 90 percent in the outright position trade. Unfortunately, few commodity traders recognize the actual potential for profits in spread trading. The key is the low, low margins which result from decreased volatility but which yield high profits on a percentage basis when favorable spread moves develop.

THE THREE TYPES OF SPREADS

While there are several hundred spread opportunities available to the futures trader at any one time, all fall under three general categories. The three types of spreads are as follows:

1. *The interdelivery or intramarket spread.* The most common type of spread, this involves the purchase and sale of different delivery months of the same commodity. For instance, long June hogs, short December hogs would qualify as an interdelivery spread.

2. *The intercommodity spread.* Intercommodity spreads consist of a long and short position—usually, but not always, in the same delivery month—of two different but related commodities. The commodities must be related to qualify as a spread for the purpose of reduced spread margins and commissions. This would disqualify such non-related commodities as, for instance, T-bills spread against broilers or pork bellies spread against gold. Corn spread against oats, hogs spread against pork bellies, or lumber spread against plywood, however, would all qualify as intercommodity spreads.

3. *The intermarket spread.* Intermarket spreads consist of long and short positions in the same commodity but in different markets. The most common intermarket spreads involve spreads between Chicago, Kansas City, or Minneapolis wheat.

THE CONCEPT OF THE GENERAL RULE

The General Rule is the most reliable and proven method of placing spreads. It applies to interdelivery spreads exclusively and is based on sound fundamental reasoning. It says simply: *in rising markets, nearby futures contracts will rise faster than distant futures contracts; and, in declining markets nearby contracts will fall faster than distant contracts.* Because the nearbys tend to be more sensitive to the basic price trend, spreaders must take care to see that their positions are placed properly. To capitalize on the tendency of the nearbys to rise faster in bull markets and fall faster in declining markets than the more distant months, the spread trader can place *bull* and *bear* spreads, respectively. A bull spread consists of a long nearby contract and a short more distant contract. A bear spread consists of a short nearby and a long distant—the opposite of the bull spread. Thus a bull spread in corn might be long May 1985 against a short July 1985. A corn bear spread in the same months would be just the opposite— short the May 1985 against long the July 1985. There are no bull or bear spreads in intercommodity or intermarket spreads because they generally are placed in the same month. In those commodities, you simply go long the more bullish commodity and short the more bearish one.

The General Rule tends to work in *some* commodities because of the relationship of the nearby month to the cash commodity. Because the nearby will soon become the cash commodity, it shares its price action. A sudden tightness in supply of the cash will translate into increased demand for the nearby as buyers bid up the price in pursuit of a real or imagined shortage in the actual commodity. Likewise, an abundant supply in the cash commodity will spill over into the nearby futures, resulting in a certain softness in the market for futures of near-term delivery. Looking toward the back months, the supply and demand equation becomes much less clear because the fundamental situation has a much longer time to come into focus. So, as a rule, the back months will follow the near months with the nearer and more active months showing the price leadership. Another term for the bull spread is *forward spread* when the long position is initiated in the nearby; and another term for the bear spread is *back spread* when the long position is initiated in the back or more distant months. Some bull and bear spreads can also be called *intercrop spreads*. This is just a specialized type of interdelivery spread in which the months of one crop year are spread against the months of another crop year. These intercrop spreads tend to be much more volatile than *intracrop* spreads and the margin requirements frequently reflect the enhanced risk.

The General Rule does not apply to every commodity traded in the futures market, but rather to those commodities that are traded in so-called *carrying charge* markets. In such markets, the normal pricing structure is dictated by the cost of carrying the commodity—insurance, storage cost, interest, and the like—from one month to another. Therefore, if the cost of carrying soybeans is 9¼ cents per month, the *full carry* or total amount that one month will exceed another month by will be 9¼ cents multiplied by the number of months that separate the two contracts. On rare occasions, the price relationship between two futures contracts will approach full carry with the nearer month selling under the more distant months in a stair-step fashion reflecting the total amount of carrying charges. More often, the nearer month will be selling in a so-called *normal* market at something less than full carry. And almost never will the nearer month sell under the more distant months by more than full carry. The reason for this last statement is that it wouldn't be economically prudent to have March soybeans selling under May soybeans for more than the cost of carrying charges. Why? Because when prices get "out of line" in this fashion, speculators need only hold the March beans to maturity, take delivery, and then retender, or resell, the March beans against a short sale in the May futures. By doing so their profit would be assured, since the cost of carrying the commodity would be less than the price difference reflected in the market when the March/May relationship exceeded full carry. In fact, speculators would do just that if the price difference between contracts exceeded the cost of carrying charges—and the two months would soon be brought back into line.

THE LIMITED-RISK SPREAD

Because of the unlikelihood of a price relationship of different months of the same commodity ever exceeding full carry, you could say there is a limit on how far a nearer month can fall below a more distant month—or how far it can widen out to full carry. This aspect of the futures market is a very important concept because it means *spreads can be initiated in so-called normal markets* (with the nearby selling below the distant month) *at comparatively little risk.* It is the underlying reason why so-called *limited-risk spreads* are so attractive. Essentially, a bull spread placed in a carrying charge market can only widen out to full carry (a negative move which would be unfavorable to the spread) but it can narrow and move away from full carry—toward the distant month and even exceeding it in a *premium* market—indefinitely. Thus the downside risk is limited while the upside potential is unlimited—a virtually unparalleled opportunity that is rarely exploited by the majority of futures traders.

Lest you grow eager to go out and find such a limited-risk spread, remember that such attractive situations aren't applicable in every commodity and that very special circumstances must prevail before such a spread can be placed at truly limited risk. The commodities that follow the General Rule, upon which the limited-risk spread is based, are as follows:

corn	sugar
wheat	cocoa
soybeans	orange juice
soybean meal	copper
soybean oil	pork bellies

There are two conditions under which the General Rule may not be applicable to these commodities, which the successful spread trader will keep clearly in mind. The first is when one of the months spread is the *spot* or delivery month. If you are trading a November-January orange juice spread during November, for instance, you may run into trouble, because a spot month near expiration can move independently or even contrary to the direction implied by the General Rule. In addition, trading limit restrictions are typically removed during the spot month, which often makes for extreme price volatility just prior to expiration. And, of course, there is always the problem of holding onto the position too long and being faced with a delivery notice. This won't result in 15,000 pounds of frozen concentrated orange juice being trucked up to your front door, but it will mean the problems of retendering or reselling the orange juice. A second problem area which would cause the spread to work counter to the General Rule would result if government intervention in the form of price controls were placed on the market. Most probably, this would have the impact of severely limiting a price rise of the nearby or soon-to-be-cash commodity while permitting the back months to rise to levels dictated by supply and demand. This artificial distortion in the supply and demand relationship would no doubt wreak havoc with spread relationships and prove a disaster to eager longs in the nearby months.

You should also be aware of the tendency of some commodities to conform to the *inverse of the General Rule*. These commodities—silver and platinum are the most notable examples—tend to show strength in the back months in rising markets and weakness in the back months in declining markets, the exact opposite pattern displayed by commodities adhering to the General Rule. Because these commodities that trade according to the inverse of the General Rule have distant months that gain relative to the more nearby contracts in a rising market and lose relative to the nearby positions in a declining market, the bull spreader buys the distant and sells the nearby. For example, if you are bullish in potatoes, you would buy May and sell the nearer March contract. The contra-normal spread pattern in potatoes derives from a combination of the pronounced seasonality of production and the high perishability of the commodity. May will invariably command a premium over more nearby contracts, and, in seasons when supplies seem inadequate, the implications are for the tightest market conditions to exist late in the season, around the time the May goes off the boards. Active buying in the May contract will often cause that month to go to an extreme premium over March and April, resulting in handsome profits for the bull spreader who understands the contra-normal spread pattern in potatoes.

In applying the General Rule, the spread trader must understand that some commodities are neither here nor there in terms of the rule, but rise or fall according to the underlying fundamentals for the respective months rather than following a general pattern. Typically, these commodities fall into the category of non-storable foods that are highly perishable. As a result of their perishability, you can't rely on carrying charges being of importance in determining price relationships. You can't, for instance, take delivery of April cattle and store them for delivery against the December contract. The same is true of the other perishable commodities such as live hogs or pork bellies. When these commodities are ready for the market they must be consumed and cannot be placed in storage to await more favorable prices.

In a sense, the perishables, therefore, are like different commodities in every contract month. April hogs will be influenced by a somewhat different set of supply and demand factors than October hogs, June cattle will differ from October cattle. The price of each contract month will depend on the market's perception of the supply and demand situation prevailing at some point in the future. In fact, it is not unusual for a Cattle on Feed report to carry bearish implications for the nearbys and bullish implications for the more distant months. The risks—and profit opportunities—inherent in trading a spread position in a perishable commodity should be evident. Theoretically, you can be long and short and lose money on *both* legs of the spread; on the other hand, both positions could be generating profits, making the spread on a non-storable commodity more profitable than an outright position. Fortunately, there are some guidelines for placing these high-risk spreads, and the seasonal factors tend to favor moves by certain months at specific times during the year.

THE SEASONAL SPREAD

Nothing is more important to the consistent profitability of spread trading than the impact of seasonal influences upon price patterns. Seasonal patterns develop as a result of cyclical supply and demand conditions that affect almost every commodity. In the most general sense, commodities tend to be high priced just prior to the harvest, when the cash commodity may be in scarce supply. During and after the harvest, as the supply picture improves and the new crop comes onstream, prices tend to be soft. Each commodity contract tends to have its own individual pattern which, when put to the test of a historical price analysis, often yields a fairly consistent period of rising and declining prices. When compared with one or more other months, a single commodity contract's price action will often reveal a seasonal pattern. And, when tested over a period of years, a contra-seasonal pattern in a spread may also be discerned.

One method used to tell whether a normal or contra-normal seasonal pattern is developing is to rely on the concept of the *critical month.* According to this concept, a spread *must* exhibit certain price behavior during a certain month of the year for a given seasonal pattern to prevail. Conversely, when prices fail to adhere to the general pattern during the critical month, a contra-seasonal stance is often suggested. Typically, the price action during the critical month will dictate the trend of the spread to the end of the crop year. For this reason, knowing the critical month and what to look for becomes an important aspect of spread analysis.

In the soybean meal market, the most reliable seasonal spread is a long January-short May meal position placed *after* the low in the critical month of October occurs. However, if the October low is violated or if the month of October passes and no definitive trend change in favor of strength in the January contract has occurred, the probability is that the spread will not work. Thus, the price behavior in the month of October is critical to how the January-May meal spread will work. Interestingly enough, this spread is critical as a bellwether of how the rest of the soybean complex will perform as well. The history of the January-May meal spread reveals that exceptionally large profits can be made by placing a bull spread during the month of October. The ideal point to place the spread is at even money (no spread difference) or when January is trading at a slight premium to May.

There are dozens of seasonal spreads available every year. Even the most reliable, however, are given to an occasional contra-cyclical move, so you shouldn't ever think of a seasonal spread—or any other for that matter—as a sure thing. The best seasonals are the result of a readily definable and understandable fundamental condition that exists year after year. And often the best are found by going back over a number of years—usually five to seven in today's markets—and measuring the tendency of, say, June hogs to rise during September and October versus the tendency of December hogs to rise during the same period. You may find that June tends to gain on December during the fall months 5 times out of 7—and that would be the basis of a sound seasonal spread. The next step would be to attempt to find the critical month. For instance, after analyzing the data, you may find that in every year, June hogs went to a premium over December hogs during September. This would make September the critical month, the month when the future movement of the spread would be decided. In the chapters that follow, a greater emphasis on how and why seasonals occur, together with specific corroborating data, will be given.

HOW TO EXPRESS A SPREAD DIFFERENCE

Spread trading has received an undeserved reputation of being complex simply because of the different ways a spread can be expressed. For instance, the typical broker will quote you a figure of so-many-points with one month over or under. This gets confusing because so-many-points one month over is the same thing as so-many-points another month under.

Let's say you are long May 1985 soybean meal at 134.40 and short August 1985 soybean meal at 142.80. The spread difference is 840 points. But to simply say 840 points isn't enough because it doesn't tell you whether the May or August contract is trading at a premium. Thus the broker might use the term, "840 points May under." This explains the exact relationship. But so does the expression "840 points August over." After awhile it gets very confusing to have to keep remembering which month is at a premium and which at a discount. To avoid all this, there is a very simple solution: *Always express the two months in terms of the long month minus the short month.* By doing so, you will always want the number to become more positive to move in your favor. For example, in the illustration below, the May '85 - August '85 soybean meal would yield a difference of −840 points (134.40 − 142.80 = −840). Any improvement in the spread (the long month gaining on the short month) would result in a more positive number—even if that more positive number were still a negative number, such as −690. Then, by taking the difference between where the spread was placed and the new price level, you can obtain the change in the spread immediately. Let's say the May meal moves to 127.30 and the August meal to 136.40. The long May has now moved a total of 710 points and the short August has moved a total of 640 points (142.80 − 136.40 = 640). The spread has moved unfavorably, since the profit on the long position is less than the gain on the short position. By how much? By the difference between where the spread was placed and its current differential. The calculations are as follows:

		Current		
Initiated:	May meal at 134.40	Price:	May meal at	127.30
−	August meal at 142.80	−	August meal at 136.40	
	− 840			−910

The total difference between −840 and −910 is −70 or $70 per spread.

Another way to look at the calculations is simply to add up the profits and losses on the respective legs as follows:

Bought one May meal at 134.40	Sold one August meal at 142.80
Sold one May meal at 127.30	Bought one August meal at 136.40
Loss: −7.10	Profit: +6.40

$$6.40 - 7.10 = -.70$$
$$70 \text{ points} = -\$70$$

All the interdelivery and intermarket spreads are expressed in terms of points or cents—the units of the two contracts spread being identical in size. But when you trade intercommodity spreads, you run into difficulty in expressing the spreads as so-many-points or cents apart because often the *two contracts differ in size.* Here's why this is a problem. If you express a spread solely as a given price difference and the underlying contracts are not identical in size, the meaning of the one cent move, or whatever, will differ according to which commodity is purchased and which sold. For example, let's say you were spreading feeder cattle against live cattle. The feeder cattle contract is 42,000 pounds while the live cattle contract is 40,000 pounds. A one cent move in the spread will be worth either $420 or $400, depending upon the direction of the move and which commodity is long or short. Moreover, if you have a one cent move in both commodities, you will have either gained $20 (the difference between $420 and $400, the value of a one cent move in either commodity) or lost $20. To avoid confusion, it helps to do one of two things: either *balance* the total size of both legs of the spread by purchasing and selling multiple contracts or use a *money spread* which simply involves expressing the spread difference in terms of the total value of the two positions. It is impractical to balance a feeder cattle-live cattle spread because the two contracts are so close in size. But other intercommodity spreads such as live cattle-live hogs do lend themselves to this approach. Since live cattle trade in a contract unit equal to 40,000 pounds and live hogs trade in a contract unit of 30,000 pounds, you can equalize the two legs of the spread by taking 3 cattle for every 4 hogs. By doing so, you will have 120,000 pounds of commodity on each leg of the spread, making a move of any magnitude in either direction comparable.

An easier approach is simply to get into the habit of thinking in terms of the money spread any time you buy and sell contracts of dissimilar specifications. It should be noted that this is an absolute must when you spread commodities that are quoted in different units altogether, such as soybeans (cents per bushel) against

against soybean meal (dollars per ton), soybean oil (cents per pound) against soybean meal, or silver (cents per troy ounce) against gold (dollars per troy ounce). To express a money spread you determine the total value of each contract by multiplying the market price by the size of the contract and then take the difference between the two. For example, you spread a long October 1985 live cattle against a short October 1985 feeder cattle. You do this because you think the feeder cattle is overpriced in terms of the live cattle and that feeders will fall relative to live, or at least not rise at a comparable rate. If you know that the price of the live cattle is 71.95 cents and the price of the feeder cattle is 85.07 cents, you have all the information you need to determine the spread differential. The calculations would be as follows:

$$
\begin{array}{lll}
\textit{October live cattle} & 71.95 \text{ cents x } 40{,}000 = & \$28{,}780 \\
\textit{October feeder cattle} & 85.07 \text{ cents x } 42{,}000 = & -\$35{,}719 \\
\hline
& \text{live cattle} - \text{feeder cattle} = & -\$\ 6{,}939
\end{array}
$$

For a profit to result in this spread, the spread difference would have to grow more positive. Let's assume that both contracts fall as anticipated, but feeder cattle declines faster than live. Since the spreader is short the feeder, a profit should result, making the money spread more positive. We'll assume the live falls a little less than 10 cents, to 62.13, and the feeder falls about 13 cents, to 72.00 cents. The calculations would appear as follows:

$$
\begin{array}{lll}
\textit{October live cattle} & 62.13 \text{ cents x } 40{,}000 = & \$24{,}851 \\
\textit{October feeder cattle} & 72.00 \text{ cents x } 42{,}000 = & -\$30{,}240 \\
\hline
& \text{live cattle} - \text{feeder cattle} = & -\$\ 5{,}389
\end{array}
$$

As you can see, the spread difference has grown more positive, signifying a profitable move in the spread.

The spread profit will be the difference of the two differentials, or $1,550 before commissions. Had the spread been liquidated at a more negative number than $-\$6{,}939$, however, a loss would have been sustained. Looking for a more positive number to develop, whether you use a conventional or money spread, is an easy way to determine where you stand in a spread and eliminates all the problems associated with using the "over" and "under" designation.

A listing of those intercommodity spreads that should be treated as money spreads is as follows:

feeder/live cattle   soybean meal/corn
cattle/hogs   soybeans/meal/oil
pork bellies/hogs   gold/silver
platinum/gold
currency spreads

THE TWO-DAY RULE

There are three key elements to every spread trade—selection, timing, and money management. The two-day rule is simply a timing tool to help you enter and exit the market at a judicious time. It will not prevent you from incurring losses; indeed, it will probably result in a number of small losses. But no good trading tool can ever avoid market mistakes no matter how well thought out. What the two-day rule will do, however, is help keep you out of the market when your timing is wrong. And once in the market, it will either minimize your losses before they grow large or protect your profits once they are achieved. The rule is based upon market momentum. The entry rule is as follows: *only place a spread when it has moved favorably on two consecutive closes.* This means you won't be able to select the very top or bottom day in a spread. Rather, the spread will already be moving in the direction you anticipate before it is placed. In general, the rule calls for putting on the spread at the close on the second consecutive day it moves in your favor. To use the rule, you will have to monitor the spread and keep a record of its closing prices. Should you not get the spread placed on the day of the second favorable close, place it on the opening of the following day. Let's see how this might work in practice. If you remember our way to express a spread as a plus or minus number, you'll understand that a favorable movement in the spread (a profitable movement) is always indicated by a more *positive number.* So you will always look for this as the key. For example, consider the following six day record of a hypothetical May-August soybean spread:

	Day 1	Day 2	Day 3	Day 4	Day 5	Day 6
May-August soybeans	-20½¢	-16¢	-19¢	-22¢	-14¼¢	-7¢
Plus/Minus		+	-	-	+	+

To begin, as you may remember, the spread difference is simply the long month minus the short month. On day 1 in this example the May soybeans were trading 20½ cents below the August soybeans—hence the minus designation. Now, as you move to the close on day 2, you will see that the spread moved more positive to − 16 cents. The two-day rule would call for the spread being initiated. Moving ahead, however, the spread then widened by three cents on day 3 and another three cents on day 4. On day 5, however, the positive direction in the spread was again evident as it moved to $-14\frac{1}{2}$ cents and the close on day 6 at -7 cents suggested that the spread be taken at that price. Looking back, it might be suggested that day 4 was actually the ideal day to initiate the spread because it was on that day that it traded at the extreme. And given the luxury of excellent hindsight, this would be correct. But at the time there was no solid indication that the spread wouldn't drift more negative, resulting in losses. For this reason, it is best to allow the movement in the spread to dictate your action. This rule does not work all the time, but it does help improve the odds in your favor.

There are two uses of the two-day rule in exiting a trade. The first says: *liquidate a spread on the second consecutive day of unfavorable price movement when the breakeven point is threatened.* This rule is designed to take you out of the market with a small profit or loss in the event the spread turns around and begins to move against you. As you may know, the most critical time in any commodity trade is just after it is initiated. Typically, if the price momentum doesn't carry the spread into a profitable position almost immediately, the chances are you will be whipsawed.* This rule was also developed to put into practice the market dictum, "Cut your losses and let your profits ride." Assuming we took the May-August soybean spread at -7 cents, let's consider the price action of the next six days below:

	Day 7	Day 8	Day 9	Day 10	Day 11	Day 12
May-August soybeans	-10¢	-12¾¢	-11¢	-8¼¢	-5¢	-8¢
Plus/Minus	-	-	+	+	+	-

After taking the spread at a price difference of -7 cents, the spread turned negative, widening to -10 cents the following day and $-12\frac{3}{4}$ cents the day after. The second consecutive day of negative movement (day 8) would have marked the liquidation signal. As you can see in the example, day 8 was the worst time to exit the market since the spread subsequently moved more positive for three consecutive days. Of course, at the time, you would have had no way of knowing this. Thus, the two-day rule, when used as a protective stop-loss technique, does occasionally result in needless losses. To remedy this drawback, you may want to rely on a standard stop-loss order placed so-many-points or cents away from your entry level.

---

* A "whipsaw" is a rapid sawing motion in price that develops when a market first turns one way and then another, typically resulting in losses for both longs and shorts whose stop-loss orders are triggered by the fluctuating market.

The second use of the two-day rule calls for *liquidating a spread on the second consecutive day of unfavorable price movement after the 100 percent profit point has been reached.* The 100 percent profit point is based on the amount of required margin. For instance, let's assume the required margin is $700. This means you want at least a 14 cent favorable movement in a grain spread before you will again apply the two-day rule. As long as the spread stays between breakeven (or a little better than breakeven to help pay for commissions) and a 100 percent profit, you will not use a stop. Of course, should the nearby month approach maturity, you will have no alternative but to liquidate the spread at the best possible market price.

If we assume that the spread moved favorably as soon as it was placed on day 6 at −7 cents, we would look for the 14 cent move (equal to $700 per spread) or +7 cents as our initial goal. Once that point is reached, we look for a reversal in the spread to signal the liquidation order. Let's consider the following price action.

	Day 7	Day 8	Day 9	Day 10	Day 11	Day 12
May-August soybeans	-10¢	-6¢	+13¢	+13½¢	+12¢	+11¢
Plus/Minus	-	+	+	+	-	-

In the above sequence of prices, the spread moved negative for one day and then rebounded sharply to +13½ cents, well above the 100 percent profit point. On day 11, however, the spread showed signs of weakness and moved more unfavorably on the following day. This second consecutive decline in the spread, after the 100 percent profit point had been reached, signalled the liquidation point on the close of day 11. Again the two-day rule did not signal the top of the spread, but it did get the trader out with a considerable profit after the momentum had changed directions.

In using the two-day rule, it is not always easy to define what constitutes a significant positive or negative move. For instance, is a move from +4 cents to +4½ cents really a significant one? Probably not. Unfortunately, there is no easy way to determine what constitutes a truly significant move. As a rule, minimum price ticks are not significant and should be treated as an unchanged market condition. In calculating a spread difference, it is important that you use closing prices. This is because spreads frequently get out of line on an intra-day basis and fluctuate widely during a trading session.

CHARTS

A spread chart reveals the price history of the spread in a way that a series of numbers on a piece of paper cannot. For this reason, it is best to get into the habit of subscribing to a chart service or keeping your own charts. There are a number of ways that a spread can be expressed on a chart, but perhaps the best is the *close-only chart.* The close-only chart shows the actual spread difference and how it changes from day-to-day and week-to-week. The chart is generated by actually taking the spread difference between two contracts and plotting the closing difference as a single point against the vertical axis and moving along the horizontal axis as time progresses. A typical close-only chart is shown in Figure 1.

As you can see, the individual points are connected by a line, resulting in a graphic portrayal of the spread's history. Such a chart can be compared with charts for the comparable spread the year before. It can also be used to identify other key chart patterns* such as support and resistance zones, trendlines, tops and bottoms and other "technical" signs.

By taking the long month and subtracting the short month, the resultant difference will always be a positive or negative number—or zero, which will mean the two contracts are trading at the same price. A positive number will mean the long month is trading above the short month—that is, the long month is the premium month and the short month the discount month. A negative spread difference will mean just the opposite—and the short month is trading above the long month and is the premium month. Whether or not the spread is initiated at a positive or negative difference is unimportant as long as it moves more positive. The direction the spread moves alone will determine its profitability. In money spreads (when two contracts of unequal sizes are spread), the chart will depict the difference in the total value of the two commodities. For example, if you are trading a hogs-cattle spread and the former commodity is worth $15,000 and the latter $20,000, your spread difference (long minus short) will be − $5,000. But if the months are reversed, the spread difference will suddenly become + $5,000, since cattle are trading above the hogs.

Some spread charts consist of two contract months plotted against one another, such as May sugar plotted along with July sugar. The relationship of the two months in this type of chart will be revealed by the widening or narrowing space between the two contracts. Spreads can also be plotted by using point-and-figure charts, which stress how far each positive or negative move carries while ignoring the time element involved.

---

* For a full explanation of charting and charting techniques, see Chapter 8 of my previous book, *Winning in the Commodities Market* (Doubleday & Co., Inc., Garden City, N.Y., 1979).

Figure 1
CATTLE/HOGS
(L Aug 84 Cattle - S Aug 84 Hogs)

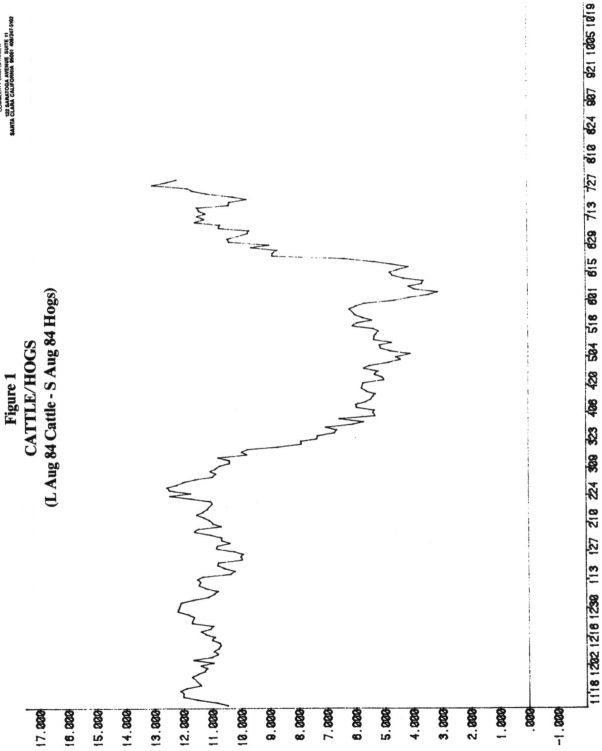

HOW TO SELECT A SPREAD TRADE

In the pages that follow, accurate historical data on carefully selected spreads is given. But before you decide on taking any spread trade, a quick check of the following rules is in order. These guidelines will alert you to the most promising spread trades *before* you apply a more rigorous analysis. Chances are, if you follow them carefully, you will turn up that "hidden" spread trade that other speculators have somehow overlooked. The rules are as follows:

1. In non-perishable commodities look for limited-risk spreads trading near full carry. As we've already mentioned, the limited-risk spread is one of the best trades available to the commodities speculator. Unfortunately, such a trade that is truly limited in risk is a rare occurrence. The reason? Aggressive traders routinely place the spreads in anticipation of bullish developments and the two months stop widening far short of full carry. Occasionally, however, a limited-risk spread will present itself simply because so few traders think the commodity has any real chance for price appreciation. These are the spreads that offer good risk/reward ratios. Don't be afraid to place a spread when the price outlook is bleak—*if* it meets the requirements of a genuine limited-risk spread and is trading near full carry. At most, your risk is the cost of commissions plus the difference between the market price and full carry.

2. Look for situations in which two contracts are "out of line." The difficulty with this rule is that it is sometimes hard to determine when two contracts are truly "out of line." Two contracts may typically trade at even money during most years, with one month going to a premium only during times of extreme disturbance in the supply and demand situation. If you miss the spread when it first starts to move, be assured that normality will again reign. This will give you an opportunity to "take the other side" of the spread and ride it back to even money. A knowledge of historical price levels and relationships can help you pinpoint a spread that has gotten out of line.

3. Pay attention to seasonality. Due to harvest pressure and other considerations that occur on a periodic basis, seasonals are among the most reliable patterns in the commodity market. A brief check of the spread's history, and a knowledge of when the spread's "critical" month occurs, will frequently yield a pattern that will indicate when the time is propitious to take a spread. The material contained in chapters that follow should give you the information you need to pinpoint the seasonal pattern.

4. Look for special situations. The big spread profits are made when something "special" happens to cause one contract or commodity to run when another is relatively sluggish. The 1979 runaway bull market in cattle presented one such special situation, and the high premium the feeder cattle achieved over the live cattle presented another. While these special situations are not exactly frequent, they occur with sufficient regularity to warrant investigation by spread traders looking for big money winners.

Part I

Interdelivery Grain Spreads

Chapter 2

Soybeans

Soybeans have been called the "Cinderella" crop, the brightest part of U.S. agriculture for 30 years. One of the most exciting commodities you can trade, soybeans are subject to wide, volatile price swings and are highly sensitive to inflation and the fluctuating value of the dollar. The soybean crop is the second largest in the United States and the leading dollar earner among U.S. exports. Harvested from September to November, the crop must fill the requirements for meal and oil until the following fall. As a result, it is then price rationed for the remainder of the year. Typically, the size of the carryover, which varies from year to year, is a key price factor. In recent years, the size of the Brazilian crop and rumors concerning that crop have had an important impact on soybean prices.

Popular with spreaders, soybeans offer a wealth of opportunities to the astute speculator. The "old-crop, new-crop" spreads are especially noted for their seasonal moves that can return excellent profits on low margins.

JULY VS. NOVEMBER SOYBEANS

This "old-crop, new-crop" soybean spread is probably the most volatile and most popular of any soybean spread. Chief among its attractive features is its profitability as both a "bull" and "bear" spread. That is, the spread is best initiated as a long July-short November spread in the fall months and held into the following spring. It is then liquidated and *reversed*—long November-short July—and held until just before the expiring July contract goes off the boards. Traded in an aggressive fashion, the spread can return profits on both sides.

43

Soybeans

It is important to note that we are talking about July and November soybeans for the same calendar year although they represent two different crop years. Thus, July is always the nearer month or "old-crop" beans, and November is the back month or "new-crop" beans. The spread should be initiated in one calendar year and carried into the next. For instance, if you were reading this in June 1985, you would be interested in trading the July 1986 and November 1986 contracts.

For the spread to work you must look for "old-crop" July beans to rise over "new-crop" November beans. Once the spread works in one direction, you then reverse positions—go long November and short July—and hold the spread until just prior to expiration. This is the typical seasonal move. In contra-seasonal years, the nearer July contract already has a large premium to November and you must put on the bear spread—long November, short July—to profit from the eventual narrowing in price between the two months. Thus there are two key strategies for using the spread: in normal-seasonal years, you want to use first a bull and then a bear spread; and in contra-seasonal years, you want to use just the bear spread alone.

As a rule, the "big" years in the spread will not follow one another consecutively, but rather appear at three to four year intervals. The reason for this is that high prices tend to encourage farmers to plant a big new crop—and this, in turn, has a softening effect on prices the following year when the record-level supplies become available. A year or two of lower prices will then provide an economic incentive for farmers to switch into other, more lucrative crops, and the supply will again tighten, resulting in a potential runaway bull market.

If you look at Table 1, you'll see that while the bull market of 1972-73 returned over $25,000 per spread, it wasn't until 1977—four years later—that the spread again made a truly sizeable move. Four years later, the pattern repeated itself once again.

Table 1
SOYBEANS
L July - S November

	Most negative difference			Most positive difference		
__Year__	__Date__	**Spread Price Difference**	__Date__	**Spread Price Difference**	**Gain From Low to High**	**Spread Value**
1971-72	Dec. 8, 1971	+ 15¼¢	Apr. 14, 1972	+ 39½¢	24¼¢	$ 1,212
1972-73	Oct. 17, 1972	+ 18¾¢	Jun. 4, 1973	+ 533¢	65½¢	$25,712
1973-74	Jul. 2, 1974	− 3½¢	Sept. 7, 1973	+ 62¢	65½¢	$ 3,275
1974-75	Jul. 22, 1975	− 4½¢	Nov. 18, 1974	+ 89¢	93½¢	$ 4,675
1975-76	Jun. 29, 1976	− 21¢	Nov. 14, 1975	− 5½¢	15½¢	$ 775
1976-77	Jul. 14, 1977	− 11¢	Apr. 22, 1977	+ 309½¢	320½¢	$16,025
1977-78	Feb. 15, 1978	+ 4½¢	Mar. 27, 1978	+ 123¼¢	119¢	$ 5,950
1978-79	Jun. 14, 1979	− 16¢	Feb. 21, 1979	+ 85¢	101¢	$ 5,050
1979-80	Mar. 31, 1980	− 40¢	Sept. 21, 1979	+ 21½¢	61½¢	$ 3,075
1980-81	Jun. 29, 1981	− 45¢	Nov. 5, 1980	+ 164½¢	209½¢	$10,475
1981-82	Feb. 26, 1982	− 19½¢	Jul. 15, 1982	+ 4½¢	24¢	$ 1,200
1982-83	Jul. 20, 1983	− 33¢	Nov. 5, 1982	+ 14½¢	47½¢	$ 2,385
1983-84	Jun. 28, 1984	+ 7¼¢	Sept. 12, 1983	+ 210½¢	203¼¢	$10,162
1984-85	Jan. 4, 1985	− 8¼¢	Aug. 16, 1984	+ 60¢	68¼¢	$ 3,412

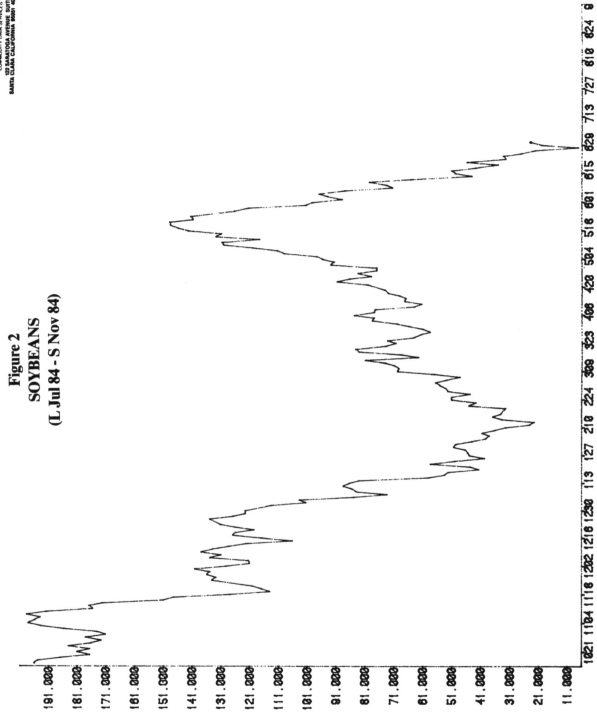

Figure 2
SOYBEANS
(L Jul 84 - S Nov 84)

Figure 3
SOYBEANS
(L Jul 83 - S Nov 83)

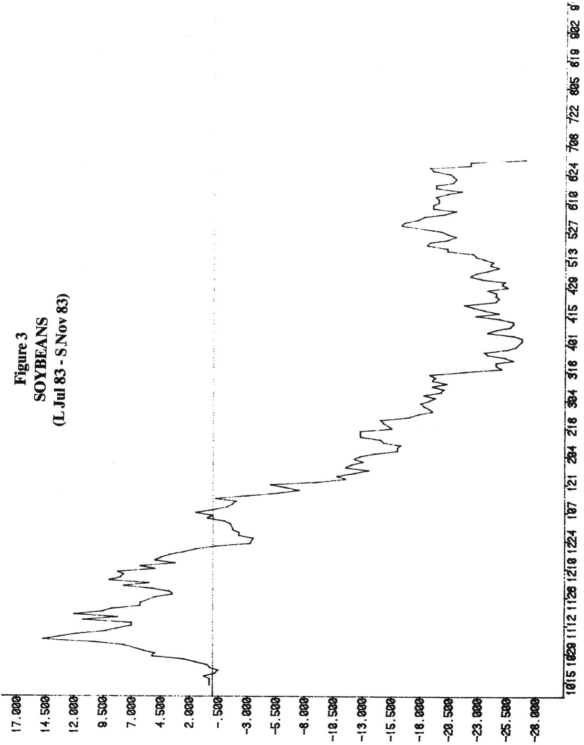

Soybeans

Typically, the spread is best initiated in the October-December period and liquidated during the following April or May; in 1978-79, however, the spread peaked early, rising to its extreme July premium during February. The seasonal pattern has been for the respective lows and highs to occur earlier and earlier, rising from the low points earlier in the fall to their subsequent highs earlier in the spring.

The big move in this intercrop spread is made in bull markets with the spread moving from close to even money in the fall to a large premium (or positive number) of July over November in the spring. In 1977, prices were propelled by trader expectations that exports and crushing would account for all "old-crop" beans, an expectation that drove July to a premium of 309½ cents over November—the largest such rise in the spread in four years. The 1977 move suggests that when supplies are tight in old-crop beans, the July contract can—and often does—rise dramatically as buyers bid higher and higher prices for supplies on hand.

One important factor that the speculator in this spread must contend with is the market's attitude toward the Brazilian soybean crop, which is generally harvested during the North American spring. Brazil is a major exporter of soybeans, and a failure in the Brazilian crop will have an inevitable bullish effect on bean prices on the Chicago Board of Trade. To enjoy maximum participation in the bean market when the Brazilian crop is a major factor, some traders shift the long leg of the spread back to the May contract. As a result, they then have one leg in the nearby month, which is apt to be the most volatile and the one likely to rise fastest should Brazil be unable to deliver a crop close to the original estimate.

Seasonal strategy. Although we've selected the end of November as the best time to place this spread, you should start considering it as early as the beginning of October. Ideally, the spread should be initiated near even money, with July holding a slight premium. A carrying charge spread might entail less risk, but the likelihood of such a spread moving up sharply is just not as good. In major bull markets—the kind you need for the spread to work—look for July to gain on November almost immediately after the October-November period. The next positive sign will be the spread's ability to close over the January highs. By the time this second confirming signal occurs, you are usually already in a nice profitable position and it is merely a question of when the spread should be liquidated. As a rule, in a normal-seasonal market, look to liquidate the spread by May at the latest, since it normally drifts more negative as the July maturity date approaches. To capitalize on this tendency to drift negative in the late spring, reverse your position and hold the bear spread through the end of June.

Contra-seasonal strategy. The key to a contra-seasonal spread working is a high July premium in the fall months. In the 1973-74 market, July was at a 39 cent premium to

November in the month of September; and, in the following year, July had attained twice that premium—89 cents over the distant November during mid-November. A large July premium early in the fall or late summer should be taken as a sign that a contra-seasonal move is in the works. When the premium of July over November exceeds 35 cents (+ 35 cents) early in the trading history of the spread, reverse positions and go long November beans and short July beans.

RULES

1. Normal seasonal. Place a long July-short November soybean spread during the month of October or November. Take profits from late March to late May—and then reverse positions and liquidate the spread on the last trading day in June. In the results shown below and on the following page, we used November 26 as the initiation date and April 22 as the liquidation date for the bull spread. The following bear spread was initiated on April 22 and closed out on June 29.

2. Contra-seasonal. When the July contract has a premium in excess of 35 cents over November (+ 35 cents) during the early weeks of each contract's trading, place a bear spread—long November-short July soybeans. Close out the position on the last trading day in June. The results shown are based on an initiation of the bear spread during the previous fall when the two contracts first began trading. The liquidation date falls on the following June 29.

Even a casual observer of the grain markets in recent years would recognize the need for the contra-seasonal strategy. Despite occasional rallies, the grain markets have been in the doldrums for the past five years. As a result, the contra-seasonal strategy has been a consistent winner since 1980 and the normal-seasonal strategy a consistent loser. In high premium markets, such as 1980-81 and 1983-84, the premiums have tended to decline substantially or disappear altogether as bearish influences pushed prices lower. Moreover, even discounted markets have slipped to still greater discounts in this spread. In the absence of inflation and abundant grain supplies, one has to bet with the contra-seasonal influences. However, the day will come when inflation will again push grain prices higher. When that day comes, the big money will be made in the traditional normal-seasonal pattern, long the intercrop July beans and short the intercrop November beans.

The profit bonanza from just over $7,000 in profits in the contra-seasonal strategy in the 10-year period ending 1979 to over $20,000 at the beginning of 1985 reflects the advisability of the contra-seasonal strategy. At the same time, the normal seasonal strategy endured losses.

SOYBEANS
L July - S November
NORMAL-SEASONAL STRATEGY

Year	Nov. 26 Initiate Spread at	April 22 Liquidate Spread at	Maximum Adversity	Maximum Profitability	Gain/Loss	Spread Value
1971-72	+ 19½¢	+ 34-7/8¢	− $ 213	+ $ 1,000	+ 54-3/4¢	+ $ 768
1972-73	+ 42¢	+185-1/8¢	− $ 113	+ $ 7,882	+143-1/8¢	+ $ 7,157
1973-74	+ 22¢	+ 18-1/2¢	− $ 675	+ $ 713	− 3-1/2¢	− $ 175
1974-75	+ 72¢	+ 16-1/4¢	− $3,525	+ $ 525	− 55-3/4¢	− $ 2,788
1975-76	− 8¢	− 16-3/4¢	− $ 450	+ $ 13	− 8-3/4¢	− $ 438
1976-77	+ 61½¢	+309-1/2¢	− $1,275	+ $12,400	+248¢	+ $12,400
1977-78	+ 25¾¢	+ 78-1/2¢	− $1,075	+ $ 4,875	+ 52-3/4¢	+ $ 2,638
1978-79	+ 44¾¢	+ 45¢	− $ 488	+ $ 2,013	+ 1/4¢	+ $ 13
1979-80	− 15¾¢	− 36¢	− $1,213	+ $ 75	− 20-1/4¢	− $ 1,013
1980-81	+123¼¢	− 31-1/2¢	− $7,963	+ $ 113	−154-3/4¢	− $ 7,738
1981-82	− 10¢	− 12¢	− $ 475	− $ 675	− 2¢	− $ 100
1982-83	+ 5¢	− 24-1/2¢	− $1,588	+ $ 200	− 19-1/2¢	− $ 1,475
1983-84	+134¼¢	+ 80¢	− $5,588	+ $ 300	− 54-1/2¢	− $ 2,713
1984-85	+ 7¾¢	+ 4-1/2¢	− $ 800	+ $ 338	− 3-1/4¢	+ $ 163*

36% Correct in 14 Years

137½¢ Net Profit

$6,875 Net Profit

---

*Day-out February 8, 1985 most recent data available

SOYBEANS
L November - S July
CONTRA-SEASONAL STRATEGY

Year	Sept. - Nov. Initiate Spread More Negative Than - 35¢	June 29 Liquidate Spread at	Maximum Adversity	Maximum Profitability	Gain/Loss	Spread Value
1971-72	− 27¼¢	No Trade	—	—	—	—
1972-73	− 27½¢	No Trade	—	—	—	—
1973-74	− 39¢	+ 2½¢	− $ 100	+ $2,063	+ 41¼¢	+ $2,063
1974-75	− 89¢	− 9¼¢	0	+ $4,375	+ 79¾¢	+ $3,988
1975-76	+ 5½¢	No Trade	—	—	—	—
1976-77	− 61½¢	− 70½¢	− $12,400	+ $1,275	− 9¢	− $ 450
1977-78	− 18½¢	No Trade	—	—	—	—
1978-79	− 37¾¢	− 2½¢	− $ 2,363	+ $2,688	+ 35¼−	+ $1,763
1979-80	− 19¢	No Trade	—	—	—	—
1980-81	− 45¢	+45¢	− $ 5,975	+ $4,500	+ 90¢	+ $4,500
1981-82	+ 15½¢	No Trade	—	—	—	—
1982-83	+ 7¢	No Trade	—	—	—	—
1983-84	− 177½¢	− 19¾¢	− $ 1,325	+ $8,513	+ 157¾¢	+ $7,888
1984-85	− 25¢	− 4½¢	0	+ $1,663	+ 20½¢	+ $1,025*

86% Correct in 7 Years

415½¢ Net profit

$20,775 Net profit

---

*Out on February 8, 1985—most recent available data

SOYBEANS
L November - S July

NORMAL-SEASONAL STRATEGY

Year	Apr. 22 Initiate Spread at	Jun. 29 Liquidate Spread at	Maximum Adversity	Maximum Profitability	Gain/Loss	Spread Value
1972	− 34½¢	− 22-7/8¢	−$ 175	+$ 582	+ 11-5/8¢	+$ 582
1973	−180¾¢	−407-1/2¢	−$17,613	0	− 226-3/4¢	−$11,338
1974	− 18½¢	+ 2-1/4¢	0	+$ 1,038	+ 20-3/4¢	+$ 1,038
1975	− 16¼¢	− 9-1/4¢	−$ 275	+$ 425	+ 7¢	+$ 350
1976	+ 16¾¢	+ 21¢	−$ 388	+$ 213	+ 4-1/4¢	+$ 213
1977	−309½¢	− 70-1/2¢	0	+$13,025	+239¢	+$11,950
1978	− 83½¢	− 48-1/4¢	−$ 975	+$ 2,200	+ 32-1/4¢	−$ 1,763
1979	− 44½¢	− 2-1/2¢	−$ 113	+$ 3,025	+ 42¢	+$ 2,100
1980	+ 36¢	+ 33¢	−$ 500	+$ 13	− 3¢	−$ 150
1981	+ 31½¢	+ 45¢	−$ 1,063	+$ 675	+ 13-1/2¢	+$ 675
1982	+ 12¢	+ 16-1/2¢	−$ 350	+$ 225	+ 4-1/2¢	+$ 225
1983	+ 24½¢	+ 22-1/4¢	−$ 413	+$ 50	− 2-1/4¢	−$ 113
1984	− 74¢	− 19-3/4¢	−$ 3,750	+$ 3,338	+ 54-1/4¢	+$ 2,713

69% Correct in 13 Years

197¼¢ Net Profit

$9,856 Net Profit

NOVEMBER VS. SEPTEMBER SOYBEANS

The tendency for this bear spread to narrow (see Table 2) as the September delivery approaches is one of the most reliable of all seasonal spread trades. Just as July beans tend to go off the boards weak, the September contract has a similar disposition in the summer months. While not quite as profitable as the bull spread in the July-November soybean spread, the reliability factor in this spread is considerably greater. Only once in eight years has the spread failed to narrow on schedule—1976. And even in that year the spread trader would have made money. The most predictable aspect of the spread is that the September short leg will prove weak during the summer months. Selecting the date when the spread will be widest, however, is a somewhat more difficult matter. The most negative reading in the spread may occur as late as May or as early as the previous September. But the March-April period seems the most consistent time of year to place the spread.

Table 2
SOYBEANS
L November - S September

	Most negative difference			Most positive difference		
Year	**Date**	**Spread Price Difference**	**Date**	**Spread Price Difference**	**Gain From Low to High**	**Spread Value**
1968-69	Aug. 12, 1969	− 11¾¢	Dec. 6, 1968	− 5¢	5-3/4¢	$ 287
1969-70	Dec. 5, 1969	− 5½¢	Sept. 21, 1970	+ 6¢	11-1/2¢	$ 575
1970-71	Oct. 28, 1970	− 11¾¢	Sept. 15, 1971	+ 4-1/8¢	15-7/8¢	$ 793
1971-72	Apr. 12, 1972	− 19½¢	Sept. 5, 1972	− 4-3/4¢	14-3/4¢	$ 737
1972-73	Jun. 26, 1973	− 297½¢	Sept. 19, 1973	+41¢	338-1/2¢	$16,925
1973-74	Sept. 10, 1973	− 30¢	Sept. 19, 1974	+17¢	47¢	$ 2,350
1974-75	Nov. 18, 1974	− 42½¢	Aug. 27, 1975	+10-1/2¢	52-1/2¢	$ 2,625
1975-76	Sept. 21, 1976	− 4¢	July 7, 1976	+12¢	16¢	$ 800
1976-77	Apr. 20, 1977	− 97½¢	Sept. 21, 1977	+21-1/2¢	119¢	$ 5,950
1977-78	May 25, 1978	− 44¢	Sept. 18, 1978	+ 1-1/4¢	45-1/2¢	$ 2,275
1978-79	Feb. 20, 1979	− 29¼¢	Sept. 19, 1979	+19-1/4¢	48-1/2¢	$ 2,425
1979-80	Sept. 21, 1979	− 6½¢	Sept. 10, 1980	+22-1/2¢	29¢	$ 1,450
1980-81	Nov. 5, 1980	− 47½¢	July 8, 1981	+23¢	70-1/2¢	$ 3,525
1981-82	Dec. 9, 1981	−1¢	Sept. 21, 1982	+11-1/2¢	12-1/2¢	$ 625
1982-83	Nov. 8, 1982	− 5¼¢	Aug. 1, 1983	+20-1/2¢	25-3/4¢	$ 1,287
1983-84	Sept. 9, 1983	− 84¢	Sept. 19, 1984	+13¢	97¢	$ 4,850

When the September and November contracts are spread, you should always look for the absence of bullish news to bring the spread back into line. Typically, this will occur on the heels of a major bull move which resulted in an "inverted market"—one in which enthusiasm for the cash commodity has pulled the nearby months over the distant ones. Because such an inverted price configuration cannot exist for long without sustained demand or tight supplies, the spread has a tendency to fall back toward carrying charges, with September trading under November. When this occurs, the long November-short September soybean spread will have a positive number, since November will again be trading at a higher price than September. To capitalize on the tendency for bean prices to soften in the summer months, place this spread during the March-April spring months and hold it into the delivery month of September, being careful to liquidate prior to the first notice day. Aggressive traders can even play the swings in this spread, taking 15 or 20 cent profits and awaiting rallies to again put on the spread, with excellent results.

TRADING RULE

Place a long November-short September soybean spread on April 15. Liquidate the spread on September 15 on the nearest trading day.

SOYBEANS
L November - S September

Year	April 15 Initiate Spread at	Sept. 15 Liquidate Spread at	Maximum Adversity	Maximum Profitability	Gain/Loss	Spread Value
1973	−66¢	−11½−	−$11,575	+$3,800	+54½¢	+$2,725
1974	− 7¾¢	+ 1½¢	−$ 125	+$ 738	+ 9¼¢	+$ 463
1975	− 2¢	+ 7½¢	−$ 213	+$ 625	+ 9½¢	+$ 475
1976	+ 6¢	+ 4¢	−$ 163	+$ 300	− 2¢	−$ 100
1977	−82¢	−14¢	−$ 775	+$4,150	+68¢	+$3,400
1978	−31¢	+ ½¢	−$ 650	+$1,575	+31½¢	+$1,575
1979	−19¾¢	+ 2¾¢	0	+$1,350	+22½¢	+$1,125
1980	+15½¢	+19½¢	−$ 300	+$ 350	+ 4¢	+$ 200
1981	+16¾¢	+ 5½¢	−$ 738	+$ 313	−11¼¢	−$ 563
1982	+ 4½¢	+ 6½¢	−$ 138	+$ 275	+ 2¢	+$ 100
1983	+11¾¢	+ 5¾¢	−$ 313	+$ 438	− 6¢	−$ 300
1984	−26¼¢	+ 3¾¢	−$ 1,425	+$1,713	+30¢	+$1,500

75% Correct in 12 Years

212¢ Net Profit

$10,600 Net Profit

Chapter 3

Soybean Meal

As a seasonal commodity, soybean meal offers a number of attractive trading opportunities every year. Meal consumption tends to be fairly seasonal and the market is heavily dominated by trade interests who tend to place and unwind their hedges on a routine seasonal basis. Moreover, the meal price is generally closely aligned with soybean prices, that rise seasonally in the fall and decline in the summer. Exceptionally large profits can be made in meal spreads when bull moves occur in the bean complex. The ideal situation is to find a limited-risk spread with the nearby month selling at a generous discount to the back months. Once the spread is placed, the trader looks for a variety of factors—ranging from an early frost to tightness in meal stocks—to exert pressure on the long month, causing it to soar to a premium over the short back month. October tends to be the critical month in meal spreads, with that month's price action dictating whether the spread will prove a winner or loser.

In the five years since the publication of the first edition of this book, the meal spreads, like the bean spreads, have been a victim of the bear market. With meal prices falling to new life-of-contract lows, the bull spreads, understandably, haven't been working. The long March-short August meal spread has been the most notable victim of the bull market. On the plus side, the long December-short September bear spread has continued to earn consistent profits over the past five years. Over the past 13 years, this spread has earned more than $15,000 on a single spread basis. That's more than $1,000 a year on margin of approximately $400 for a position that is held less than four months.

JANUARY VS. MAY SOYBEAN MEAL

Placed in the early fall, this spread can usually be initiated with January selling at a 400 to 600 point discount to May. By the end of October, which is the critical month, the spread tends to invert and January then goes to a premium over the more distant May. As a rule, November and December will favor the spread as January, approaching maturity, continues to gain on the May contract. Because meal prices are so closely tied to bean and oil prices, look to the entire soybean complex to signal a bull move for the spread to work with the best results (See Table 3 and results).

TRADING RULE

Buy January soybean meal and sell May soybean meal on September 22. Liquidate the spread on December 22.

Table 3

SOYBEAN MEAL

L January - S May

	Most negative difference			Most positive difference		
Year	Date	Spread Price Difference	Date	Spread Price Difference	Gain From Low to High	Spread Value
1972-73	July 20, 1972	− 235	Jan. 16, 1973	+ 3790	4025	$4,025
1973-74	Oct. 24, 1973	− 400	Dec. 12, 1973	+ 1400	1800	$1,800
1974-75	Dec. 30, 1974	− 1750	Jan. 22, 1975	+ 50	1800	$1,800
1975-76	May 6, 1975	− 1750	Jan. 21, 1976	+ 520	2270	$2,270
1976-77	Jan. 18, 1977	− 520	Nov. 19, 1976	+ 340	860	$ 860
1977-78	Sept. 22, 1977	− 770	Mar. 4, 1977	0	770	$ 770
1978-79	Aug. 10, 1978	− 510	Dec. 18, 1978	+ 490	1000	$1,000
1979-80	Jan. 9, 1980	− 1080	July 17, 1979	− 30	1050	$1,050
1980-81	Dec. 17, 1980	− 2000	Aug. 6, 1980	− 100	1900	$1,900
1981-82	Sept. 16, 1981	− 1430	Jan. 15, 1982	+ 110	1540	$1,540
1982-83	June 17, 1982	− 1150	Dec. 30, 1982	+ 40	1190	$1,190
1983-84	Apr. 27, 1983	− 1020	Aug. 25, 1983	+ 250	1270	$1,270
1984-85	Nov. 6, 1984	− 1250	May 25, 1984	− 250	1000	$1,000

SOYBEAN MEAL
L January - S May

Year	Sept. 22 Initiate Spread at	Dec. 22 Liquidate Spread At	Maximum Adversity	Maximum Profitability	Gain/Loss	Spread Value
1972	− 80	+ 2820	− $ 75	− $3,010	+ 2900	+ $2,900
1973	− 190	+ 220	− $ 210	+ $1,590	+ 410	+ $ 410
1974	− 780	− 1400	− $ 750	+ $ 180	− 620	− $ 620
1975	− 550	− 240	− $ 100	+ $ 640	+ 310	+ $ 310
1976	− 150	− 190	− $ 220	+ $ 490	− 40	− $ 40
1977	− 770	− 360	0	+ $ 410	+ 410	+ $ 410
1978	− 280	+ 70	− $ 60	+ $ 770	+ 350	+ $ 350
1979	− 560	− 740	− $ 340	+ $ 370	− 180	− $ 180
1980	− 340	− 1700	− $1,660	+ $ 140	− 1360	− $1,360
1981	− 1290	− 490	− $ 100	+ $1,140	+ 800	+ $ 800
1982	− 670	− 80	− $ 90	+ $ 640	+ 590	+ $ 590
1983	− 450	− 80	0	+ $ 670	+ 370	+ $ 370
1984	− 980	− 1070	− $ 270	+ $ 160	− 90	− $ 90

61% Correct in 13 Years

3850 Points Net Profit

$3,850 Net Profit

SEPTEMBER VS. DECEMBER SOYBEAN MEAL

The bull September-December meal spread tends to work best from the early part of the year through the month of May, when it tends to move negative until the nearby September goes off the boards. Highly seasonal in nature, the spread is best reversed in May and held as a bear spread through the summer months. During the past several years, the spread has tended to top out as early as March or April, suggesting that traders must stay alert to the possibility of taking profits somewhat sooner than anticipated. Be cautioned that the spread entails considerable risk. A sudden bull move in the bean complex can cause the nearby to soar at the expense of the distant month, resulting in losses if the trader is bear spread. Such a reverse move occurred in the 1979 September-December meal spread during mid-June. But this was soon followed by the seasonal downtrend that resulted in the bear spread working after all (See Table 4 and results).

RULES

Buy September soybean meal and sell December soybean meal on January 27. Liquidate the spread on May 8 and reverse positions by selling September meal and buying December meal. Close out the long December-short September meal spread on September 4.

57

Table 4
SOYBEAN MEAL
L September - S December

	Most negative difference			Most positive difference		
Year	Date	Spread Price Difference	Date	Spread Price Difference	Gain From Low to High	Spread Value
1972-73	Sept. 14, 1973	− 870	Jun. 27, 1973	+ 13,800	14,670	$14,670
1973-74	Sept. 17, 1974	−2780	Jan. 21, 1974	+ 100	2,880	$ 2,880
1974-75	Aug. 19, 1975	− 950	Dec. 19, 1974	+ 900	1,850	$ 1,850
1975-76	Aug. 2, 1976	− 570	May 20, 1976	+ 330	900	$ 900
1976-77	Sept. 21, 1977	− 890	Apr. 22, 1977	+ 5,130	6,020	$ 6,020
1977-78	Sept. 20, 1978	− 410	Mar. 28, 1978	+ 1,250	1,660	$ 1,660
1978-79	Jun. 13, 1979	− 530	Apr. 6, 1979	+ 780	1,310	$ 1,310
1979-80	Sept. 19, 1980	− 940	Nov. 9, 1979	− 190	750	$ 750
1980-81	July 10, 1981	− 990	Oct. 29, 1980	+ 2,200	3,190	$ 3,190
1981-82	Sept. 13, 1982	− 690	Dec. 10, 1981	− 50	640	$ 640
1982-83	July 19, 1983	− 830	Sept. 21, 1983	+ 250	1,080	$ 1,080
1983-84	Sept. 4, 1984	− 920	Nov. 15, 1983	+ 2,500	3,420	$ 3,420

SOYBEAN MEAL
L September - S December

Year	Jan. 27 Initiate Spread at	May 8 Liquidate Spread at	Maximum Adversity	Maximum Profitability	Gain/Loss	Spread Value
1973	+ 2930	+ 9370	− $180	+ $6,440	+ 6440	+ $6,440
1974	0	− 530	− $800	+ $ 70	− 530	− $ 530
1975	− 400	− 280	− $390	+ $ 250	+ 120	+ $ 120
1976	− 300	− 200	− $180	+ $ 110	+ 100	+ $ 100
1977	+ 1250	+ 3350	+ $340	+ $3,880	+ 2100	+ $2,100
1978	− 20	+ 670	− $220	+ $1,270	+ 690	+ $ 690
1979	+ 290	+ 90	− $280	+ $ 490	− 200	− $ 200
1980	− 520	− 720	− $310	+ $ 150	− 200	− $ 200
1981	− 80	− 570	− $680	+ $ 30	− 490	− $ 490
1982	− 380	− 360	− $120	+ $ 140	+ 20	+ $ 20
1983	− 400	− 610	− $380	+ $ 110	− 210	− $ 210
1984	+ 220	+ 470	− $300	+ $ 320	+ 250	+ $ 250

58% Correct in 12 Years

8090 Net Points Profit

$8,090 Net Profit

SOYBEAN MEAL
L December - S September

Year	May 8 Initiate Spread at	Sept. 4 Liquidate Spread at	Maximum Adversity	Maximum Profitability	Gain/Loss	Spread Value
1972	− 750	− 320	− $ 340	+ $ 555	+ 430	+ $ 430
1973	− 9370	− 600	− $4,430	+ $8,770	+ 8770	+ $8,770
1974	+ 530	+ 1170	− $ 150	+ $ 670	+ 640	+ $ 640
1975	+ 280	+ 390	− $ 70	+ $ 670	+ 110	+ $ 110
1976	+ 190	+ 110	− $ 520	+ $ 380	− 80	− $ 80
1977	− 2930	− 180	− $1,000	+ $3,220	+ 2750	+ $2,750
1978	− 670	+ 350	− $ 360	+ $1,020	+ 1020	+ $1,020
1979	− 90	+ 380	− $ 380	+ $ 620	+ 470	+ $ 470
1980	+ 720	− 720	+ $ 120	+ $ 220	0	0
1981	+ 570	+ 490	− $ 240	+ $ 420	− 80	− $ 80
1982	+ 360	+ 440	− $ 40	+ $ 210	+ 80	+ $ 80
1983	+ 610	+ 340	− $ 700	+ $ 220	− 270	− $ 270
1984	− 470	+ 920	− $ 650	+ $1,390	+ 1390	+ $1,390

69% Correct in 13 Years

15,230 Points Net Profit

+ $15,230 Net Profit

MARCH VS. AUGUST SOYBEAN MEAL

This spread is best initiated in October as a bull spread near even money and held into the December-January period. At that point, the spread tends to stop widening and moves the other way in favor of the August meal. October is the critical month for this spread. Should prices during October favor the bull spread, the seasonal move will generally occur as anticipated (See Table 5 and results together with Figures 4 and 5).

TRADING RULE

Buy March soybean meal and sell August soybean meal on October 27. Liquidate the spread on December 31.

Table 5
SOYBEAN MEAL
L March - S August

	Most negative difference			Most positive difference		
Year	Date	Spread Price Difference	Date	Spread Price Difference	Gain From Low to High	Spread Value
1968-69	Feb. 18, 1969	− 350	Sept. 11, 1968	− 50	300	$ 300
1969-70	Nov. 24, 1969	− 300	Feb. 24, 1970	+ 1135	1435	$1,435
1970-71	Mar. 2, 1971	− 185	Jan. 4, 1971	+ 60	245	$ 245
1971-72	Feb. 15, 1972	− 230	Dec. 6, 1971	− 45	185	$ 185
1972-73	Oct. 10, 1972	− 200	Mar. 7, 1973	+ 2550	2750	$2,750
1973-74	Mar. 11, 1974	− 1470	Dec. 11, 1973	+ 850	2320	$2,320
1974-75	Mar. 12, 1975	− 1920	Oct. 18, 1974	0	1920	$1,920
1975-76	Aug. 26, 1975	− 1100	Mar. 19, 1976	− 100	1000	$1,000
1976-77	Mar. 9, 1977	− 720	Nov. 22, 1976	+ 1130	1850	$1,850
1977-78	Sept. 8, 1977	− 940	Mar. 17, 1978	+ 120	1060	$1,060
1978-79	Mar. 7, 1979	− 960	Nov. 3, 1978	+ 530	1490	$1,490
1979-80	Mar. 5, 1980	− 1820	Aug. 1, 1979	− 100	1720	$1,720
1980-81	Feb. 26, 1981	− 2030	Nov. 5, 1980	+ 1280	3310	$3,310
1981-82	Oct. 1, 1981	− 1520	Dec. 11, 1981	− 230	1290	$1,290
1982-83	Mar. 21, 1983	− 1120	Nov. 19, 1982	− 60	1060	$1,060
1983-84	Feb. 13, 1984	− 1140	Aug. 16, 1983	+ 1950	3090	$3,090
1984-85	Feb . 7, 1985*	− 1460	Sept. 18, 1984	− 580	880	$ 880

* Data available through Feb. 8, 1985

SOYBEAN MEAL
L March - S August

Year	Oct. 27 Initiate Spread at	Dec. 31 Liquidate Spreadat	Maximum Adversity	Maximum Profitability	Gain/Loss	Spread Value
1972-73	+ 5	+ 1,625	− $ 40	+ $1,720	+ 1,620	+ $1,620
1973-74	+ 250	+ 170	− $ 600	+ $ 600	− 80	− $ 80
1974-75	− 800	− 1,550	− $ 830	+ $ 270	− 750	− $ 750
1975-76	− 220	− 180	− $ 280	+ $ 90	+ 40	+ $ 40
1976-77	+ 150	+ 620	− $ 390	+ $ 310	+ 470	+ $ 470
1977-78	− 730	− 330	− $ 100	+ $ 470	+ 400	+ $ 400
1978-79	+ 300	+ 50	− $ 380	+ $ 230	− .250	− $ 250
1979-80	− 1,000	− 1,270	− $ 280	+ $ 500	− 270	− $ 270
1980-81	+ 330	− 870	− $2,080	+ $ 950	− 1,200	− $1,200
1981-82	− 1,210	− 610	− $ 10	+ $ 980	+ 600	+ $ 600
1982-83	− 300	− 200	0	+ $ 240	+ 100	+ $ 100
1983-84	+ 1,450	+ 70	− $1,390	+ $ 330	− 1,380	− $1,380
1984-85	− 1,220	− 1,260	− $ 110	+ $ 170	− 40	− $ 40

46% Correct in 13 Years

740 Points Net Loss

$740 Net Loss

Figure 4
SOYBEAN MEAL
(L Mar 84 - S Aug 84)

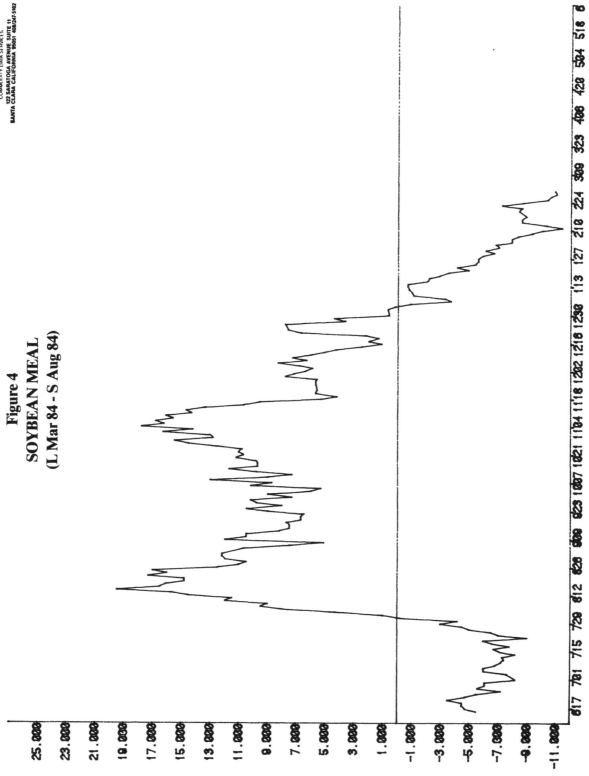

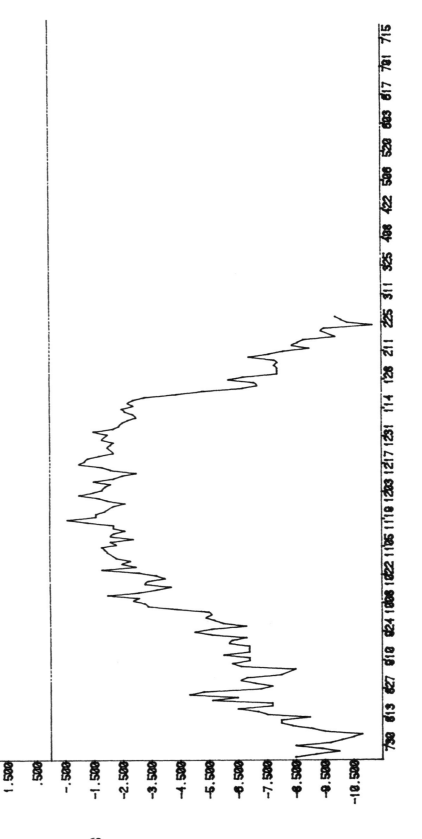

Figure 5
SOYBEAN MEAL
(L Mar 83 - S Aug 83)

Chapter 4

Soybean Oil

As one of the two products of soybeans, oil shares the seasonal patern of both beans and meal, tending to rise during the fall and winter and moving downward during the summer months. Unlike meal, which is primarily a feed grain, soybean oil is used basically as an ingredient in the manufacture of salad oil, margarine, and shortening for human use. Demand tends to remain stable and is somewhat inelastic to price. Thus the market fluctuates primarily in response to changes in supply. From a seasonal standpoint, soybean oil is, in every sense, the equal of beans and meal—rather consistently profitable for the spreader who understands the seasonal moves.

MAY VS. AUGUST SOYBEAN OIL

In this spread, the May tends to gain on the August throughout the fall months until the expiration of the May contract. In a typical seasonal move, the spread will begin to work in mid-to-late October. For our own analysis, we used October 15 as the initiation date and May 1 as the liquidation date. Similar bull spreads in adjacent months can also be used with somewhat comparable success. March-September soybean oil readily comes to mind as a spread with a similar pattern.

When the spread works—and, it should be noted, it doesn't every year—the reliability factor is quite high. In the last three seasonal moves, the initiation period proved to be the September-October period; and in the past four seasonal moves, the spread peaked during the April-May time period. You should note also that the

Soybean Oil

substantial moves in the spread ($1,500 and up per spread) occurred every time in the past seven years in a seasonal move.

October is a critical month. Look for the spread to rise above its October highs after the month is over. Such a move suggests the normal seasonal pattern will persist. A failure to rise above the October highs, however, would indicate a contra-seasonal move—such as occurred during 1979. Should the October highs not be broken, be prepared to liquidate the spread in anticipation of the contra-seasonal pattern occurring.

Should you not wish to hold the spread until the delivery month, look to take profits during January, when the spread tends to dip. The January setback in prices also offers an opportunity to add other spreads or initiate the spread should you have failed to initiate it originally during October (See Table 6 and results).

TRADING RULE

Buy May soybean oil and sell August soybean oil on October 15. Liquidate the spread on May 1 or the first trading day in May.

Table 6
SOYBEAN OIL
L May - S August

Year	Most negative difference		Most positive difference			
	Date	Spread Price Difference	Date	Spread Price Difference	Gain From Low to High	Spread Value
1972-73	Jan. 4, 1973	− 20	May 7, 1973	+ 82	102	$ 612
1973-74	Oct. 19, 1973	+ 20	Apr. 26, 1974	+ 495	475	$2,850
1974-75	Oct. 31, 1974	+ 15	Apr. 22, 1975	+ 280	265	$1,590
1975-76	Jan. 26, 1976	− 44	May 21, 1975	+ 127	171	$1,026
1976-77	Apr. 29, 1977	− 52	Nov. 17, 1976	+ 75	127	$ 762
1977-78	Sept. 26, 1977	− 35	May 1, 1978	+ 220	255	$1,530
1978-79	May 21, 1979	− 78	Sept. 19, 1978	+ 80	158	$ 948
1979-80	Apr. 7, 1980	− 104	Sept. 21, 1979	+ 30	134	$ 804
1980-81	May 19, 1981	− 142	Aug. 8, 1980	+ 22	164	$ 984
1981-82	Feb. 16, 1982	− 103	Aug. 28, 1981	− 33	70	$ 420
1982-83	Sept. 7, 1982	− 65	Nov. 4, 1982	− 10	55	$ 220
1983-84	Jun. 27, 1983	− 45	Aug. 26, 1983	+ 300	345	$2,070
1984-85	Jul. 20, 1984	− 32	Mar. 29, 1984	+ 294	326	$1,956

SOYBEAN OIL
L May - S August

Year	Oct. 15 Initiate Spread at	May 1 Liquidate Spread at	Maximum Adversity	Maximum Profitability	Gain/Loss	Spread Value
1972-73	− 5	+ 37	−$ 90	+$ 450	+ 42	+$ 252
1973-74	+ 35	+397	−$ 90	+$2,760	+362	+$2,172
1974-75	+125	+232	−$ 660	+$ 930	+107	+$ 642
1975-76	− 8	− 34	−$ 216	+$ 48	− 26	−$ 156
1976-77	+ 38	− 23	−$ 540	+$ 222	− 61	−$ 366
1977-78	− 35	+220	0	+$1,530	+255	+$1,530
1978-79	+ 43	− 24	−$ 534	+$ 174	− 67	−$ 402
1979-80	− 13	− 84	−$ 546	+$ 60	− 71	−$ 426
1980-81	0	−117	−$ 738	+$ 12	−117	−$ 702
1981-82	− 85	− 79	−$ 108	+$ 222	+ 6	+$ 36
1982-83	− 30	− 35	−$ 204	+$ 120	− 5	−$ 30
1983-84	+205	+110	−$1,362	+$ 12	− 95	−$ 570
1984-85	+ 55	+138*	−$ 240	+$ 510	+ 83	+$ 498

* Out on February 8, 1985—most recent data available

43% Correct in 14 Years
413 Net Points Profit
$2,478 Net Profit

SEPTEMBER VS. DECEMBER SOYBEAN OIL

A year rarely passes when there isn't a sharp run up of September over December soybean oil. The pattern tends to parallel that of September-December meal. While the spread may make its move as early as the first of the year, sometimes patience is called for, since the bull move may not occur until late May. Fortunately, the return is frequently worth the wait. In recent years, the tendency has been for the spread to reach its maximum peak of September over December earlier in the year (See Table 7 and results, together with Figures 6 and 7).

TRADING RULE

Buy September and sell December soybean oil one year out when the contracts first start trading. Liquidate the spread on May 15.

Soybean Oil

Table 7
SOYBEAN OIL
L September - S December

	Most negative difference			Most positive difference		
Year	Date	Spread Price Difference	Date	Spread Price Difference	Gain From Low to High	Spread Value
1972-73	Oct. 13, 1972	+ 3	Aug. 23, 1973	+1,107	1,104	$6,624
1973-74	Dec. 18, 1973	+ 43	Aug. 2, 1974	+ 504	459	$2,754
1974-75	Sept. 3, 1975	+ 31	Jan. 3, 1975	+ 358	327	$1,962
1975-76	Aug. 13, 1976	− 54	Sept. 21, 1976	+ 45	99	$ 594
1976-77	Sept. 21, 1977	− 97	May 16, 1977	+ 354	451	$2,706
1977-78	Nov. 2, 1977	− 10	Mar. 28, 1978	+ 279	289	$1,734
1978-79	Jun. 14, 1979	− 19	Sept. 14, 1979	+ 282	301	$1,806
1979-80	Aug. 28, 1980	− 91	Oct. 8, 1979	+ 10	101	$ 606
1980-81	July 27, 1981	− 149	Nov. 19, 1980	+ 160	309	$1,854
1981-82	Feb. 16, 1982	− 80	Nov. 24, 1981	− 25	55	$ 330
1982-83	Sept. 15, 1983	− 120	Sept. 21, 1983	+ 90	210	$1,260
1983-84	Jan. 20, 1984	+ 10	May 18, 1984	+ 545	535	$3,210
1984-85	Oct. 3, 1984	− 1	Feb. 5, 1985*	+ 175	174	$1,044

* Data available through February 8, 1985

SOYBEAN OIL
L September - S December

Year	When First Trading Initiate Spread at	May 15 Liquidate Spread at	Maximum Adversity	Maximum Profitability	Gain/Loss	Spread Value
1973-74	+ 68	+213	−$ 150	+$1,056	+ 145	+$ 870
1974-75	+310	+140	−$1,332	+$ 288	− 170	−$1,020
1975-76	− 5	− 33	−$ 168	0	− 28	−$ 168
1976-77	+ 15	+354	−$ 168	+2,034	+339	+$2,034
1977-78	+ 20	+192	−$ 180	+1,554	+172	+$1,032
1978-79	+ 75	+ 17	−$ 348	+$ 732	− 58	−$ 348
1979-80	− 24	− 53	+$ 330	+$ 84	− 29	−$ 174
1980-81	+ 85	−105	−$1,248	+$ 450	− 190	−$1,140
1981-82	− 55	− 54	−$ 150	+$ 180	+ 1	+$ 6
1982-83	− 46	− 51	−$ 126	+$ 246	− 5	−$ 30
1983-84	+250	+485	−$1,440	+$1,410	+235	+$1,410
1984-85	+ 43	+165*	−$ 258	+$ 792	+122	+$ 732

* Through February 8, 1985—most recent data available

50% Correct in 12 Years
534 Points Net Profit
$3,204 Net Profit

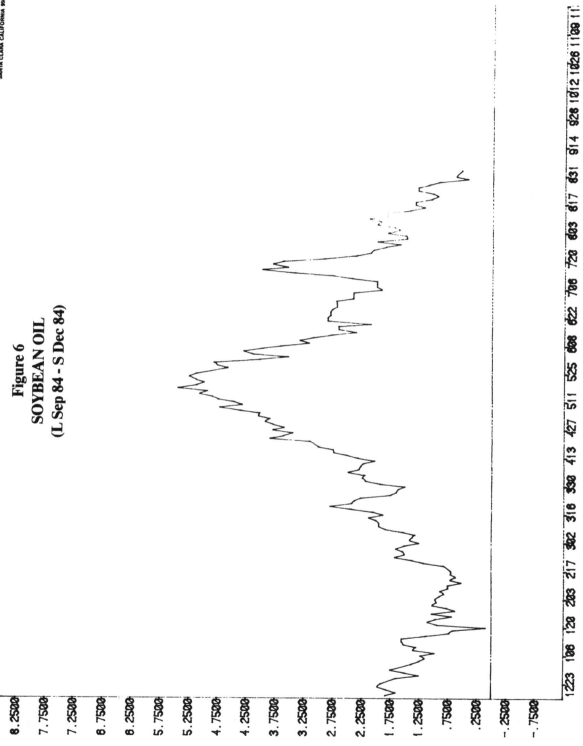

Figure 6
SOYBEAN OIL
(L Sep 84 - S Dec 84)

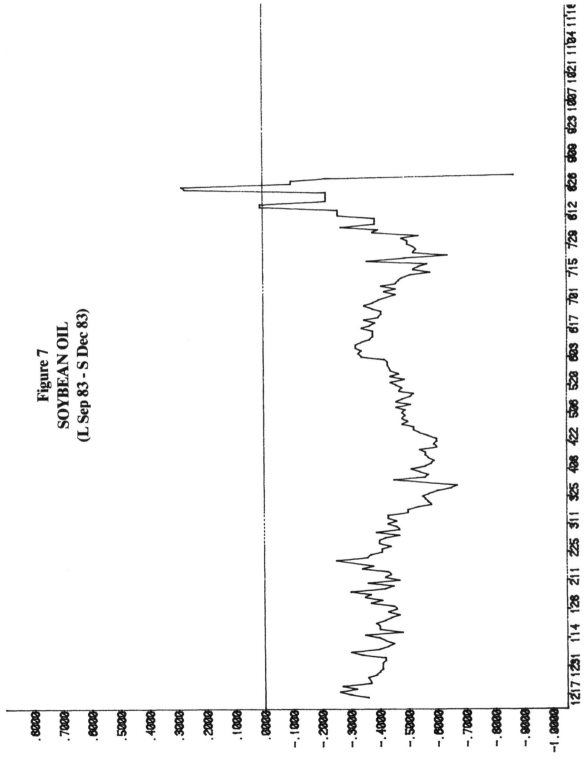

Figure 7
SOYBEAN OIL
(L Sep 83 - S Dec 83)

Chapter 5

Corn

Like the other grains, corn has a very well-defined seasonal pattern based upon the commodity's growing season. The corn crop year runs from October 1 to the following September 30, with the month of October being the principal month of harvest. While corn has a very complex pricing mechanism, the major components of the supply-demand equation consist of the weather on the supply side and the demand for animal end-products on the demand side. July and August are the critical weather months for corn. Higher than normal rainfall during the summer months favors higher yields and lower prices. Below normal rainfall, especially during July, adversely affects yields and favors higher corn prices. Excessive temperatures in the corn-growing regions in the Midwest during August can also have a negative impact on yields and serve to boost corn prices.

From the demand side, corn's role in our economy is primarily that of a feed grain for beef, hogs, and poultry. About 90 percent of the corn grown in the United States is used as animal feed and the demand for the animal end-products, especially beef cattle, is vital to the demand for corn.

In recent years, corn crops have broken records in 1976, 1977, and 1978. Corn prices have been maintained primarily due to a combination of government support programs and unprecedented strong demand for corn as a feed grain both domestically and abroad.

Corn

DECEMBER VS. JULY CORN

It is important to understand that the spread we are talking about here involves contract months in the *same* calendar year—December 1985 corn, for instance, spread against July 1985 corn, December 1986 corn against July 1986 corn, and so on. Thus the July contract will expire before the December contract. Typically, the spread will be placed when the distant December contract first commences trading, about October of the previous year. If past performance is any indication that the spread will result in profits in the future, the reliability factor in this spread is very high. In the past six years, the December contract has shown a tendency to gain ground on the July contract from the fall months into the spring, and sometimes right up to the expiration of the July contract. During the month of October, the long December, short July corn spread can generally be put on with December trading at a sharp discount to July. By the following spring or summer, the discount has disappeared about 50 percent of the time and December has gone to a premium over July; or, at the very least, the December discount will have lessened considerably. One nice feature of this spread is its tendency to work in both bull and bear markets. One word of caution is due, however. During the April-May period, the spread will occasionally move back in favor of the July. When this happens, the aggressive trader should reverse positions and hold the spread until the first day of trading in the July delivery month (See Table 8 and results, together with Figures 8 and 9).

TRADING RULE

Place a long December, short July corn spread on October 15. Liquidate the spread on April 15. Be certain to spread the distant December, more than a year out, against the nearer July contract.

Table 8
CORN
L December - S July (same calendar year)

	Most negative difference			Most positive difference		
Year	Date	Spread Price Difference	Date	Spread Price Difference	Gain From Low to High	Spread Value
1973-74	Sept. 25, 1973	−44¼¢	July 22, 1974	−12¢	32¼¢	$1,612
1974-75	Oct. 7, 1974	−68¾¢	Mar. 3, 1975	−18¢	50¾¢	$2,537
1975-76	Oct. 7, 1975	−26½¢	April 20, 1976	− 3¾¢	22¾¢	$1,137
1976-77	Oct. 6, 1976	−18¢	July 5, 1977	+12¾¢	30¾¢	$1,537
1977-78	Dec. 8, 1977	− 4¾¢	July 18, 1978	+13½¢	18¼¢	$ 912
1978-79	Nov. 15, 1978	+ 1¾¢	July 14, 1979	+14½¢	12¾¢	$ 637
1979-80	Sept. 27, 1979	+ 2½¢	Mar. 12, 1980	+21¼¢	18¾¢	$ 937
1980-81	Nov. 14, 1980	−37¼¢	July 8, 1981	+22½¢	59¾¢	$2,987
1981-82	July 16, 1982	− 9¾¢	Feb. 26, 1982	+13½¢	23¼¢	$1,162
1982-83	July 8, 1983	−51¼¢	Dec. 9, 1982	+15½¢	66¾¢	$3,337
1983-84	July 16, 1984	−69½¢	Feb. 14, 1984	−37½¢	32¢	$1,600
1984-85	Sept. 24, 1984	−18¼¢	Dec. 4, 1984	− 4¼¢	14¢	$ 700

CORN
L December - S July (same calendar year)

Year	Oct. 15 Initiate Spread at	April 15 Liquidate Spread at	Maximum Adversity	Maximum Profitability	Gain/Loss	Spread Value
1972-73	−13½¢	− 3-1/8¢	−$ 75	+$ 518	+10-3/8¢	+$ 518
1973-74	−23¾¢	−16-1/2¢	−$ 663	+$ 463	+ 7-1/4¢	+$ 363
1974-75	−48¢	−24¢	−$ 563	+$1,500	+24¢	+$1,200
1975-76	−24¼¢	− 4-1/2¢	−$ 50	+$ 988	+19-3/4¢	+$ 988
1976-77	−15½¢	+ 7-1/4¢	0	+$1,200	+22-3/4¢	+$1,138
1977-78	+ 2¢	− 2¢	−$ 338	+$ 138	− 4¢	−$ 200
1978-79	+ 6¼¢	+ 5-3/4¢	−$ 225	+$ 175	− 1/2¢	−$ 25
1979-80	+ 6¼¢	+16-3/4¢	−$ 75	+$ 750	+10-1/2¢	+$ 525
1980-81	−23¼¢	+ 9-1/4¢	−$ 700	+$1,825	+32-1/2¢	+$1,625
1981-82	+ 9¢	+ 7¢	−$ 300	+$ 225	− 2¢	−$ 100
1982-83	+12¢	−15¢	−$1,475	+$ 175	−27¢	−$1,350
1983-84	−53¢	−52-1/2¢	−$ 150	+$ 775	+ 1/2¢	+$ 25
1984-85	− 7¾¢	−11-3/4¢*	−$ 338	+$ 175	− 4¢	−$ 200

62% Correct in 13 Years
90-1/8¢ Net Profit
$4,506 Net Profit

---

* Through February 8, 1985—most recent data available

71

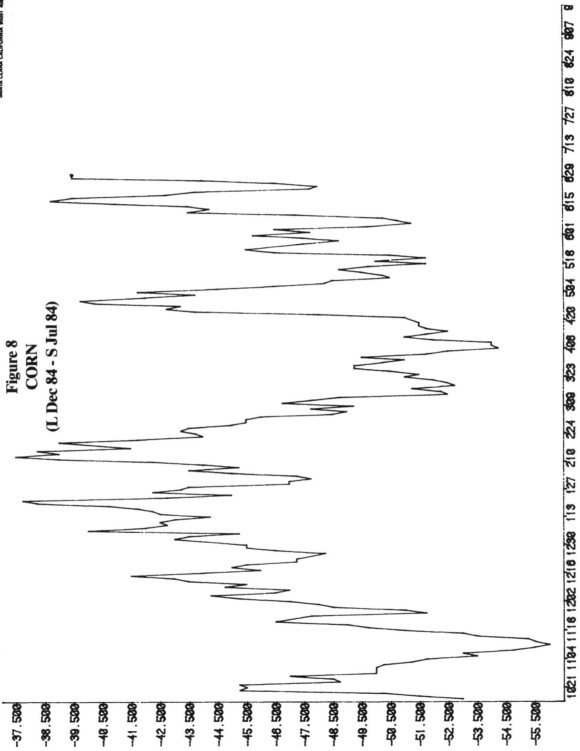

Figure 8
CORN
(L Dec 84 - S Jul 84)

72

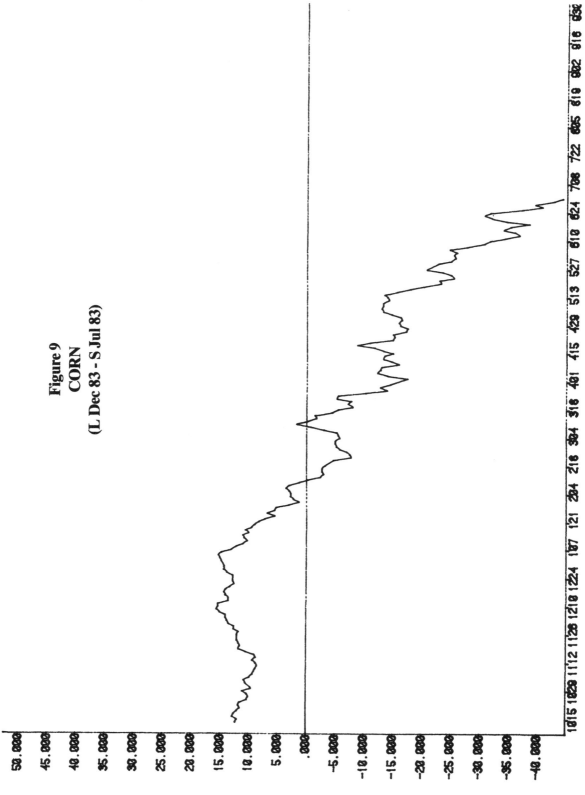

Figure 9
CORN
(L Dec 83 - S Jul 83)

73

Corn

DECEMBER VS. SEPTEMBER CORN

This same calendar year spread parallels the price action in the December-July corn spread, with the exception that it can generally be held somewhat longer. Although the spread didn't work in 1979, the previous five years, as well as 1980, all show nice seasonal moves from the fall into the following summer, with December gaining ground on the September contract (Table 9 and results follow).

TRADING RULE

Initiate a long December, short September corn spread on October 15. Liquidate the spread on September 1 or the first trading day of the delivery month. As with the previous spread, be careful to place the spread in the distant December contract against the nearer July contract.

Table 9

CORN

L December - S September (same calendar year)

	Most negative difference			Most positive difference		
Year	Date	Spread Price Difference	Date	Spread Price Difference	Gain From Low to High	Spread Value
1973-74	Sept. 25, 1973	−35¢	Sept. 19, 1974	+ 6¢	41¢	$2,050
1974-75	Oct. 7, 1974	−44½¢	Aug. 22, 1975	+ 1¢	45½¢	$2,275
1975-76	Oct. 16, 1975	−14½¢	Aug. 30, 1976	+ ½¢	15¢	$ 750
1976-77	Oct. 13, 1976	− 9½¢	Sept. 21, 1977	+10¢	19½¢	$ 975
1977-78	Nov. 10, 1977	− 2¢	Sept. 20, 1978	+11¾¢	13¾¢	$ 687
1978-79	Aug. 8, 1979	− 4¾¢	June 14, 1979	+ 7½¢	12¼¢	$ 612
1979-80	Sept. 2, 1980	− 2¾¢	July 15, 1980	+10¾¢	13½¢	$ 675
1980-81	Nov. 13, 1980	−23¢	Sept. 15, 1981	+20¢	43¢	$2,150
1981-82	Sept. 21, 1982	− 7¼¢	Aug. 13, 1982	+ 8¢	15¼¢	$ 762
1982-83	July 5, 1983	−26¾¢	Sept. 21, 1983	+14¼¢	41¢	$2,050
1983-84	Aug. 23, 1983	−32¢	July 30, 1984	− 7¾¢	24¼¢	$1,212

CORN
L December - S September (same calendar year)

Year	Oct. 15 Initiate Spread at	Sept. 1 Liquidate Spread at	Maximum Adversity	Maximum Profitability	Gain/Loss	Spread Value
1972-73	− 11¼¢	+ ¾¢	− $ 738	+ $ 600	+ 12¢	+ $ 600
1973-74	− 21¢	− 2¼¢	− $ 438	+ $ 938	+ 18¾¢	+ $ 938
1974-75	− 30½¢	− ¼¢	− $ 625	+ $1,575	+ 30¼¢	+ $1,513
1975-76	− 13¢	− 1¾¢	− $ 75	+ $ 675	+ 11¼¢	+ $ 563
1976-77	− 9¢	+ 9¢	0	+ $ 938	+ 18¢	+ $ 900
1977-78	+ 1½¢	+ 8¾¢	− $ 175	+ $ 363	+ 7¼¢	+ $ 363
1978-79	+ 4½¢	− ½¢	− $ 463	+ $ 150	− 5¢	− $ 250
1979-80	+ 3¢	− 2¾¢	− $ 288	+ $ 388	− 5¾¢	− 288
1980-81	− 11¾¢	+ 14¾¢	− $ 563	+ $1,325	+ 26½¢	+ $1,325
1981-82	+ 4¾¢	+ 2½¢	− $ 338	+ $ 163	− 2¼¢	− $ 113
1982-83	+ 7¼¢	+ 2½¢	− $1,700	+ $ 113	− 4¾¢	− $ 238
1983-84	− 23¼¢	− 9¢	− $ 125	+ $ 775	+ 14¼¢	+ $ 713

67% Correct in 12 Years
120½¢ Net profit
$6,025 Net profit

Chapter 6

Wheat

Wheat has a complex pricing structure that is influenced by production levels, export demand, the size of the carryover, and government support programs. In addition, wheat prices can be influenced by the cost of substitute feed grains—an added factor that makes a fundamental analysis particularly difficult. Government reserve programs have the impact of making more supplies available when prices are high and supporting the market when supplies are abundant. Nevertheless, the commodity is subject to a seasonal pattern that occurs with sufficient regularity to warrant investigation. The most popular wheat spreads are May vs. July and December vs. May. These two wheat spreads alone can be held about nine months out of the year. Speculators in the May-July wheat spread tend to go long the "old crop" May and short the "new-crop" July during the summer months. The spread is then held until winter and reversed when the May begins to lose on July. Any shortages, such as occurred during 1978, will cause the "old-crop" May wheat to be in demand and close above July as it approaches maturity.

DECEMBER VS. MAY WHEAT

Wheat resembles corn in that the December contract tends to be heavily discounted early in the calendar year and tends to gain relative to the near contract months as the year progresses. To capitalize on this tendency, the wheat should be bear spread early in the year and liquidated as the May contract approaches maturity. During 1978 and 1979, however, a series of bullish news events served to push the May to a sharp premium over December—a normal bullish pattern—and the spread failed to work. Traders should be alert to the possibility of bullish news events causing a contra-seasonal movement in this spread. In 1978, for instance, uncertain wheat supplies from Canada and Australia fueled the rumor that China would be a strong buyer of wheat from the United States. As a result wheat prices rose, with the nearer May contract stronger than the distant December. The bull move was given further impetus when the government announced it would boost the reserve level and the price that farmers would be paid to store grain. The interesting aspect of bull markets in this wheat spread is that even in the contra-seasonal years, the spread tends to collapse prior to maturity, with the nearer May going off the boards weak. Typically, this pattern is caused by the traders short hedging in the fall and lifting their hedges, by buying back their positions, in the spring. Technically weak after the short covering is over, the market experiences lower prices as the commercial trade is out of the market and the long speculators have long since taken their profits (See Table 10 and results, together with Figures 10 and 11).

Despite two lackluster years, the bear spreads in wheat have chalked up some nice profits over the past five years. Since 1980, the long December-short May wheat spread has earned more than $2,000 net on margin of just $300—a proven low-risk, money-maker. Given the weak performance of the grain market during 1984-85, this year promises to be another winner in this spread, which capitalizes on bear markets.

TRADING RULE

Buy December wheat and sell May wheat on January 15. Liquidate the spread on May 1.

Table 10
WHEAT
L December - S May

	Most negative difference			Most positive difference		
Year	Date	Spread Price Difference	Date	Spread Price Difference	Gain From High to Low	Spread Value
1969-70	May 19, 1970	− 8¢	Jan. 29, 1970	+ 1-1/4¢	9-1/4¢	$ 462
1970-71	May 19, 1971	− 15-3/4¢	Jan. 8, 1971	+ 2-3/8¢	16-1/8¢	$ 806
1971-72	May 10, 1972	− 14-3/8¢	Mar. 13, 1972	+ 1/4¢	14-5/8¢	$ 731
1972-73	Jan. 12, 1973	− 19-3/4¢	May 21, 1973	− 1/4¢	19-1/2¢	$ 975
1973-74	Feb. 19, 1974	− 79-1/2¢	May 13, 1974	+23¢	102-1/2¢	$5,125
1974-75	Oct. 14, 1974	− 33¢	May 20, 1975	+ 15-1/4¢	48-1/4¢	$2,412
1975-76	Jan. 14, 1976	+ 15-1/4¢	May 4, 1976	+ 28-1/2¢	13-1/4¢	$ 662
1976-77	Nov. 12, 1976	+ 12-1/2¢	Feb. 28, 1977	+ 30-1/4¢	17-3/4¢	$ 887
1977-78	May 19, 1978	+ 4¢	Jan. 19, 1978	+24¢	20¢	$1,000
1978-79	Mar. 5, 1979	− 16¢	May 18, 1979	+ 15-1/2¢	31-1/2¢	$1,575
1979-80	Oct. 1, 1979	− 3-1/4¢	Mar. 28, 1980	+ 48-1/2¢	51-3/4¢	$2,587
1980-81	Oct. 29, 1980	− 9-1/4¢	May 8, 1981	+ 62-1/2¢	71-3/4¢	$3,587
1981-82	Nov. 19, 1981	+ 16-3/4¢	May 7, 1982	+ 53-1/4¢	36-1/2¢	$1,825
1982-83	Nov. 5, 1982	+ 21-1/4¢	Mar. 7, 1983	+40¢	18-3/4¢	$ 937
1983-84	May 21, 1984	− 12¢	Jan. 26, 1984	+ 21-1/4¢	33-1/4¢	$1,662
1984-85	Jan. 10, 1985	− 2¢	Dec. 11, 1984	+ 10-1/2¢	12-1/2¢	$ 625

WHEAT
L December - S May (same calendar year)

Year	Jan. 15 Initiate Spread at	May 1 Liquidate Spread at	Maximum Adversity	Maximum Profitability	Gain/Loss	Spread Value
1973	− 18½¢	− 14¼¢	− $ 50	+ $ 543	+ 4¼¢	+ $ 213
1974	− 51½¢	+ 6½¢	− $1,400	+ $2,900	+58¢	+ $2,900
1975	− 6¾¢	+15	0	+ $1,088	+ 21¾¢	+ $1,088
1976	+ 17¾¢	+ 27¼¢	− $ 75	+ $ 538	+ 9½¢	+ $ 475
1977	+ 20¼¢	+ 23¾¢	0	+ $ 500	+ 3½¢	+ $ 175
1978	+ 19¾¢	+ 11¾¢	− $ 613	+ $ 213	− 8¢	− $ 400
1979	− 2¼¢	+ 2¾¢	− $ 688	+ $ 500	+ 5¢	+ $ 250
1980	+ 36¼¢	+ 46½¢	− $ 438	+ $ 613	+ 10¼¢	+ $ 513
1981	+ 24¢	+ 43½¢	− $ 138	+ $1,263	+ 19½¢	+ $ 975
1982	+ 31¼¢	+ 53¼¢	− $ 63	+ $1,100	+ 22¢	+ $1,100
1983	+ 31¼¢	+ 29¾¢	− $ 175	+ $ 438	− 1½¢	− $ 75
1984	+ 7¾¢	+ 1½¢	− $ 763	+ $ 675	− 6¼¢	− $ 313

75% Correct in 12 Years

144¾¢ Net Profit

$7,237 Net Profit

79

DATA SOURCE
COMMODITY DATA SERVICES
122 SARATOGA AVENUE SUITE 11
SANTA CLARA CALIFORNIA 95051 408/247-5102

Figure 10
WHEAT
(L Dec 84 - S May 84)

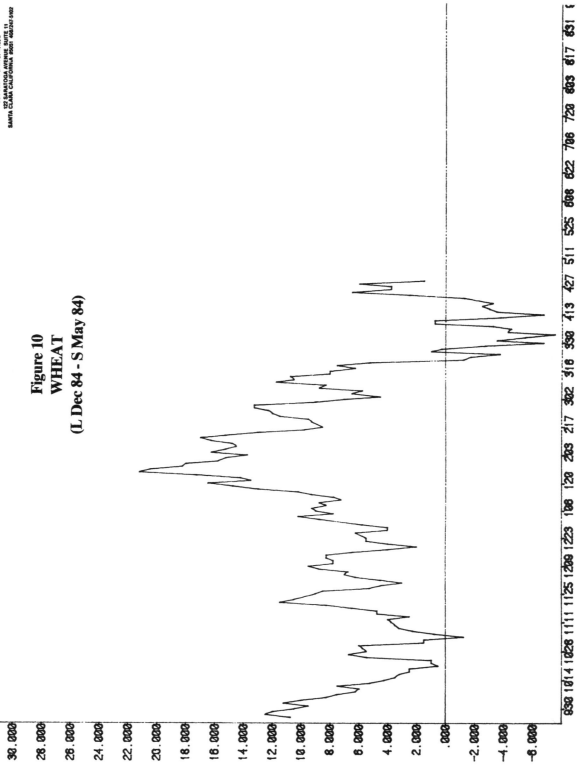

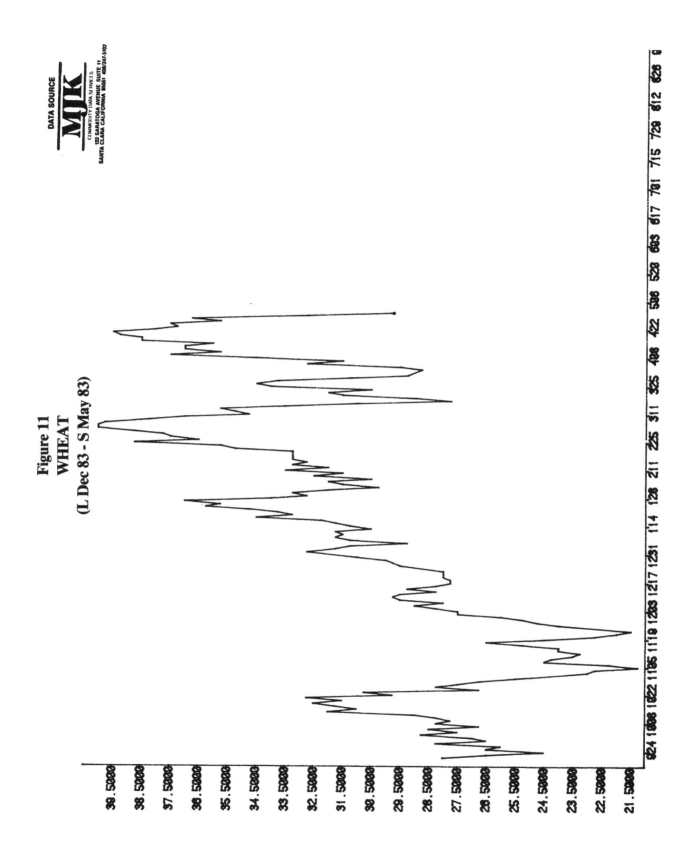

Figure 11
WHEAT
(L Dec 83 - S May 83)

Chapter 7

Oats

Oats, like corn and soybean meal, are used primarily as a feed grain. Unlike corn, however, which is harvested in the fall, the oats crop is harvested during July and the summer months are apt to reflect this fact with low prices, especially during August, the month of greatest marketing. The oats crop year runs from July 1 through June 30. Thus the July contract represents "new-crop" oats. Most heavily utilized during the fall and winter months when feed requirements are heaviest, oats can be expected to sell at their highest prices at this time. The market is highly sensitive to the weather and, due to its relative thinness compared to the other grains, the market can be moved by only a small amount of speculative activity.

JULY VS. MAY OATS

Like several of the other grains, the bear spread tends to work best in oats. Nevertheless, the commodity has a strong contra-seasonal trend that can be profitable if the spread is reversed. Typically, to catch the seasonal trend, you want to find the market inverted, with the nearer May contract selling at a premium to the more distant July during the late fall. To profit on the spread, therefore, you will want to return to a carrying charge pattern, with the May selling under the July. While the profits on the seasonal move tend to be somewhat smaller than the contra-seasonal move, they also appear to be more consistent. In the big bull markets, of course, the May contract can be expected to gain ground on July oats right through to maturity and go off the boards

Oats

strong (see Table 11 and results, together with Figures 12 and 13).

TRADING RULE

Buy July oats and sell May oats on November 30. Liquidate the spread on May 1.

Table 11
OATS
L July - S May

	Most negative difference			Most positive difference		
Year	Date	Spread Price Difference	Date	Spread Price Difference	Gain From Low to High	Spread Value
1974-75	May 20, 1975	− 33½¢	Nov. 12, 1974	+ 3	36½¢	$1,825
1975-76	Nov. 26, 1975	− 7¢	May 19, 1976	+ 3½¢	10½¢	$ 525
1976-77	May 19, 1977	− 16¾¢	Aug. 17, 1976	+ ½¢	16¼¢	$ 812
1977-78	Nov. 21, 1977	− 2¼¢	May 1, 1978	+ 8½¢	10¾¢	$ 537
1978-79	Oct. 3, 1978	− 1¾¢	Apr. 26, 1979	+ 9½¢	11¼¢	$ 562
1979-80	Aug. 31, 1979	+ 1¢	Mar. 19, 1980	+ 9¾¢	8¾¢	$ 437
1980-81	May 18, 1981	− 12½¢	May 1, 1981	+ 5½¢	18¢	$ 900
1981-82	Nov. 13, 1981	− 18½¢	Sept. 23, 1981	− 2½¢	16¢	$ 800
1982-83	July 29, 1982	− 4¢	Feb. 3, 1983	+ 9¢	13¢	$ 650
1983-84	Apr. 6, 1984	− 5¼¢	May 2, 1984	+ 7¢	12¼¢	$ 612
1984-85	Feb. 8, 1985*	− 5¾¢	Jan. 25, 1985	− 1¼¢	4½¢*	$ 225

*Data available through February 8, 1985

OATS
L July - S May

Year	Nov. 30 Initiate Spread at	May 1 Liquidate Spread at	Maximum Adversity	Maximum Profitability	Gain/Loss	Spread Value
1974-75	− 2¾¢	− 8¼¢	−$538	+ 4½¢	− $275	
1975-76	− 4¾¢	− 2½¢	−$ 75	+$175	+ 2¼¢	+$113
1976-77	− 5½¢	− 10½¢	−$475	+$113	− 5¢	− $250
1977-78	+ ½¢	+ 8½¢	−$ 75	+$400	+ 8¢	+$400
1978-79	+ 4¢	+ 8½¢	−$ 13	+$275	+ 4½¢	+$225
1979-80	+ 4¢	+ 3¼¢	−$ 25	+$288	+ ½¢	+ $ 13
1980-81	− 5½¢	+ 5½¢	−$338	+$550	+11¢	+$550
1981-82	−13¢	−14¢	−$213	+$388	− 1¢	− $ 50
1982-83	− ¼¢	+ 5¢	−$ 38	+$463	+ 5¼¢	+$263
1983-84	+ 2¢	+ 5¼¢	−$363	+$200	+ 3¼¢	+$163

70% Correct in 10 Years

23¢ Net Profit

$1,150 Net Profit

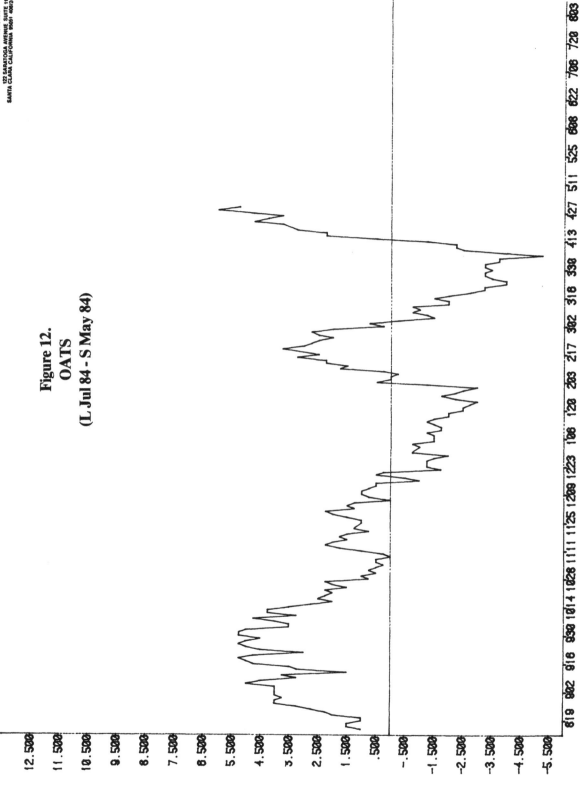

Figure 12.
OATS
(L Jul 84 - S May 84)

85

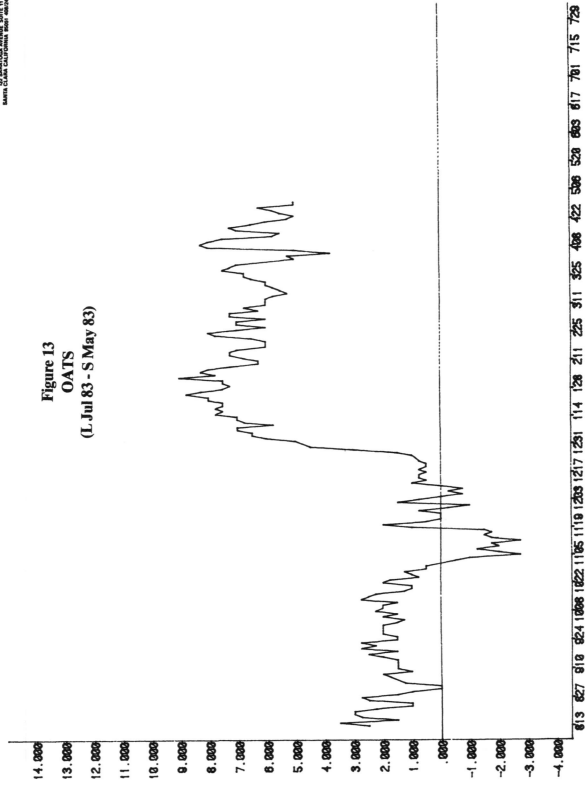

Figure 13
OATS
(L Jul 83 - S May 83)

86

Part II
Interdelivery Meat Spreads

Chapter 8

Live Cattle

As a seasonal trade, cattle offers some of the most consistently profitable spreads to be found in the futures market. Although there is no planting or harvest season for cattle, as there is for other crops, there is a period of high production when comparatively abundant supplies tend to hang heavily over the market. As a rule, demand for live cattle is strongest in mid-winter and late spring, with the greatest price strength in June or July and February. Traditionally, the meat complex moves higher early in the year and registers annual lows during the month of April.

The cattle market is characterized by comparatively few buyers and many suppliers. Since the commodity is, by definition, nonstorable, the sellers must often place their cattle on the market at prices that are not sufficient to generate a profit. The supply of the commodity is based on a multitude of factors, but an important consideration for a cattle raiser is the cost of feed grains, especially corn. In addition, supplies will depend upon how long the cattle are fed or "finished" before they are brought to market, the size of calf crops, and the level of inventories of cattle already on feed. Marketed throughout the year, cattle still have a strong seasonal period. Slaughter tends to be greatest in October and weakest in February, which tends to influence price relationships.

JUNE VS. OCTOBER LIVE CATTLE

In each of the past 20 years, the June live cattle has made progress on the distant

Live Cattle

October live cattle during the early months of the year. Exhibiting a highly reliable pattern, the long June, short October cattle spread tends to rise off its mid-January lows and move in favor of the June contract almost through to expiration. During some years, the high in the spread will be reached as early as March or April and in other years it will already be the delivery month when the most positive difference exists. But, as a rule, mid-May finds the June trading at a nice premium to October. In only two of the last 20 years has June not gone to a premium over October—1966 and 1967. And even in those years, when cattle trading was still comparatively new, the spread moved more positive during the month of February. The strongest indication that the spread will work is a June discount to October early in the year. Typically, the discounted June will then mount a rise and go to a premium over October, resulting in nice profits on this spread. Over the past 18 years, the spread has never risen less than 200 points June over October at some time during the spring. This is a highly attractive spread trade in every respect (See Table 12 and results, together with Figures 14 and 15).

TRADING RULE

Buy June live cattle, sell October live cattle on January 15. Liquidate the spread on May 15.

Table 12
LIVE CATTLE
L June - S October

	Most negative difference			Most positive difference		
Year	Date	Spread Difference	Date	Spread Price Difference	Gain From Low to High	Spread Value
1964-65	Mar. 12, 1965	− 45	May 6, 1965	+ 150	195	$ 780
1965-66	Feb. 3, 1966	− 60	Feb. 18, 1966	− 35	25	$ 100
1966-67	Feb. 3, 1967	−120	Feb. 18, 1967	− 80	40	$ 160
1967-68	Dec. 9, 1967	−115	Apr. 12, 1968	+ 165	280	$1,120
1968-69	Dec. 21, 1968	− 25	Jun. 1, 1969	+ 310	335	$1,340
1969-70	Jan. 12, 1970	+ 20	Apr. 1, 1970	+ 80	60	$ 240
1970-71	Dec. 1, 1970	+ 50	May 15, 1971	+ 270	220	$ 880
1971-72	Dec. 8, 1971	+ 35	May 25, 1972	+ 255	220	$ 880
1972-73	Jan. 23, 1973	+ 10	Mar. 15, 1973	+ 225	215	$ 860
1973-74	Feb. 25, 1974	−325	May 9, 1974	+ 220	545	$2,180
1974-75	Jan. 12, 1975	− 47	Jun. 4, 1975	+ 930	977	$3,908
1975-76	Mar. 2, 1976	−250	Apr. 14, 1976	+ 280	530	$2,120
1976-77	Jan. 5, 1977	−217	May 3, 1977	+ 260	477	$1,908
1977-78	Aug. 8, 1977	−105	Jun. 12, 1978	+ 653	758	$3,032
1978-79	Nov. 9, 1978	− 53	Mar. 22, 1979	+ 530	583	$2,332
1979-80	Apr. 18, 1980	+ 12	Jun. 19, 1980	+ 435	423	$1,692
1980-81	Jan. 29, 1981	+ 20	Jun. 11, 1980	+ 505	485	$1,940
1981-82	Sept. 16, 1981	+ 75	Jun. 17, 1982	+1287	1212	$4,848
1982-83	Nov. 26, 1982	+150	Jun. 17, 1983	+ 952	802	$3,208
1983-84	Jun. 6, 1984	+210	Feb. 29, 1984	+ 595	385	$1,540
1984-85	Aug. 17, 1984	+122	Oct. 26, 1984	+ 465	343	$1,372

LIVE CATTLE
L June - S October

Year	Jan. 15 Initiate Spread at	May 15 Liquidate Spread at	Maximum Adversity	Maximum Profitability	Gain/Loss	Spread Value
1970	+ 33	+ 15	− $ 112	+ $ 636	− 18	+ $ 72
1971	+ 70	+260	− $ 48	+ $ 848	+ 190	+ $ 760
1972	+130	+223	− $ 120	+ $ 388	+ 93	+ $ 372
1973	+167	+ 53	− $ 748	+ $ 272	− 114	− $ 456
1974	+240	+120	− $2,252	+ $ 188	− 120	− $ 480
1975	− 48	+765	0	+ $3,632	+ 813	+ $3,252
1976	− 42	−225	− $ 932	+ $1,448	− 183	− $ 732
1977	−200	+168	0	+ $1,840	+ 368	+ $1,472
1978	− 25	+180	− $ 92	+ $1,040	+ 205	+ $ 820
1979	+180	+227	− $ 268	+ $1,400	+ 47	+ $ 188
1980	+140	+137	− $ 512	+ $ 608	− 2.5	− $ 12
1981	+130	+373	− $ 440	+ $1,260	+ 242.5	+ $ 972
1982	+260	+842	− $ 48	+ $2,328	+ 582.5	+ $2,328
1983	+327	+590	− $ 448	+ $1,832	+ 262.5	+ $1,052
1984	+477	+310	− $ 668	+ $ 472	− 167.5	− $ 668

60% Correct in 15 Years

2200 Points Net Profit

$8,800 Net Profit

DATA SOURCE
MJK
COMMODITY DATA SERVICES
122 SARATOGA AVENUE SUITE 11
SANTA CLARA CALIFORNIA 95051 408/247-5102

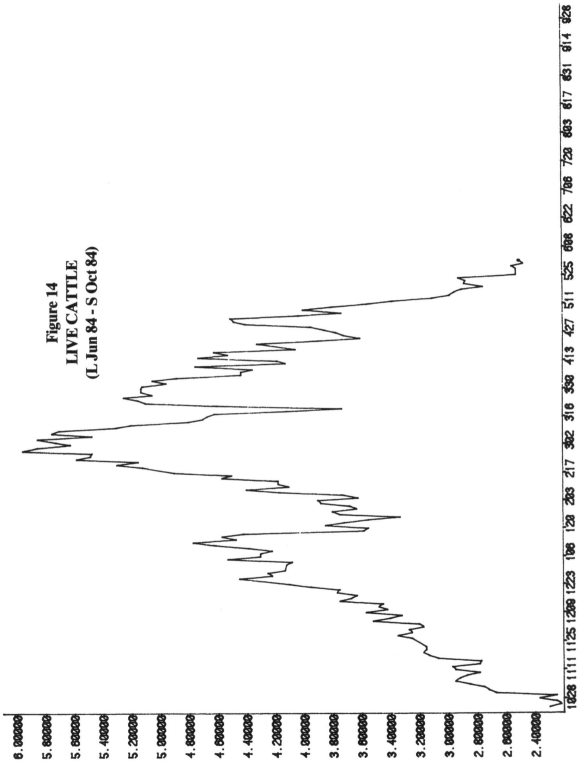

Figure 14
LIVE CATTLE
(L Jun 84 - S Oct 84)

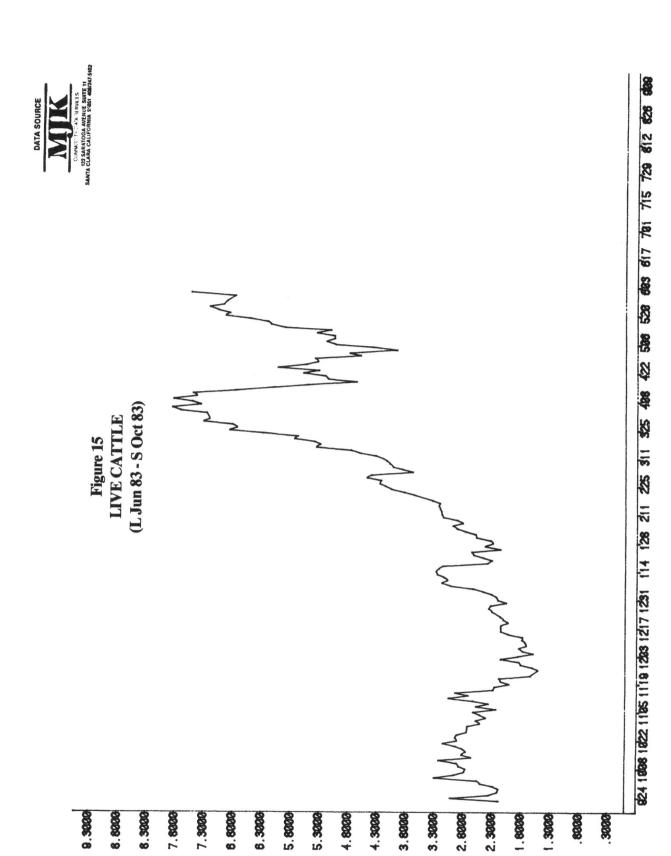

Figure 15
LIVE CATTLE
(L Jun 83 - S Oct 83)

93

Chapter 9

Live Hogs

Live hogs have a decided seasonal tendency based on a number of supply and demand factors that make spreading a very profitable activity during certain times of the year. From the standpoint of demand, pork consumption is influenced by the level of income, holiday periods, the price of pork compared to competing products, and the cost of feed grains, especially corn. As a rule, Americans tend to increase their consumption of pork during the Christmas holidays, resulting in traditional seasonal price rises at the end of the year. Being price elastic, the demand for pork also tends to rise during the early summer and fall when hog prices are apt to be their lowest.

A highly perishable commodity, hogs must be sent to market once they reach slaughter weight—often regardless of the profitability involved. For this reason, it pays for speculators and hedgers alike to understand the growing cycle that so often results in abundant hog numbers at certain times of the year and a scarcity at other times. The hog market is characterized by many independent producers who increase or decrease their breeding operations in response to two main factors—the price of feed grains, most notably corn, and the prevailing market price of hogs. Typically, low-cost grain will translate into large hog numbers. Many analysts rely on what is known as the "hog/corn ratio" to predict just what the pig crop will look like in the future. As a rule, ten months is considered the lead time for production of hogs, since a pig's gestation period is approximately 112 days and it takes about six months on feed to bring a hog to slaughter weight. The hog/corn ratio expresses the relationship of feeding costs to sales volume. It is expressed as the number of units of corn equal in value to 100 pounds of live pork. When corn, which is the primary feed for hogs, is high in price, the ratio will be low; conversely, lower corn prices will mean a higher ratio since it will take more units of corn to equal the higher corn costs than a ratio of, say, 18.7. Thus, when the ratio is high and corn costs are low, producers will tend to increase hog numbers, causing the ratio to again fall, as more pork produced results in lower hog prices. In checking back on the hog/corn ratio, a high of just over 24 during late October 1978 was followed by a steady decline in hog prices which bottomed out in late July 1979— just ten months later!—between 32 and 33 cents. The hog/corn ratio can be a good forecaster of prices. When the ratio peaks, look for hog prices to bottom ten months later. Conversely, when the ratio bottoms, look for hog prices to peak ten months later.

It should be noted that hog production is highly sensitive to price. High prices result in an abundance of hogs being brought to market—usually 10 to 12 months down the road depending on the time of year. Since the market is highly fragmented, every producer tends to think he will be able to take advantage of the high prevailing prices. Unfortunately, this is not so. Rather, large numbers of pigs brought to market only results in low prices. When this occurs, of course, producers have a disincentive to raise hogs, and the entire cycle must begin over again. While there are a variety of identifiable cycles in the hog market, the long term cycle tends to run approximately five to six years. Relatively high prices will tend to stimulate hog production for several years and then the cycle will go into reverse as the increased production leads to depressed prices, which, in turn, tends to influence producers to cut production.

Hog production, which, understandably enough, tends to be concentrated in the Corn Belt states, tends to follow a seasonal pattern. The largest number of farrowings or pig births tend to occur throughout the spring during the months of March, April and May. Given the six month lag between birth and slaughter, during which time the animals are on feed, this translates into the August through December period when the "spring pigs" are brought to market. Just as the harvest period tends to be the time of lowest prices in the grains, the large slaughter of hogs during the fall months means an abundance of the commodity and a corresponding pressure on prices. As a rule, therefore, look for the lowest-of-the-year hog prices to occur between August and December. In recent years, the cycles in hog prices have been spread out a little more, due to increasing mechanization and the breeding of hogs throughout the year. Nevertheless, the pattern still exists—with prices at their lowest in the fall. As winter approaches, hogs tend to go into a sustained bull market, rising during the first three months of the year and, sometimes, sustaining the price rise right into the summer months. Traditionally, May is a month when hogs tend to rise as much as 78 percent of the time. After May, however, prices often slip, especially around the time of the June Pig Crop report.

DECEMBER VS. APRIL HOGS

This back spread, which consists of two months of the same calendar year, has a pronounced seasonality that favors the distant December contract gaining on the nearby April in the late winter, on through maturity of the nearby April contract. Typically the spread registers its high during the month of February and then moves downward in favor of the December. To participate in this spread's seasonality, you should put on your position in late January and hold it through to the end of March—or even into the delivery month (See Table 13 and results, together with Figures 16 and 17).

TRADING RULE

Buy December hogs and sell April hogs on January 14. Liquidate the spread on March 27.

Table 13
LIVE HOGS
L December - S April (same calendar year)

	Most negative difference			Most positive difference		
Year	Date	Spread Price Difference	Date	Spread Price Difference	Gain From Low to High	Spread Value
1970	Feb. 25, 1970	− 410	Apr. 20, 1970	− 230	180	$ 540
1971	Feb. 22, 1971	+ 275	Apr. 16, 1971	+ 625	350	$1,050
1971-72	Jan. 27, 1972	− 275	Apr. 12, 1972	+ 200	475	$1,425
1972-73	Feb. 28, 1973	− 582	Mar. 27, 1973	− 150	432	$1,296
1973-74	Nov. 5, 1973	− 412	Feb. 27, 1974	+1063	1475	$4,425
1974-75	Nov. 22, 1974	− 30	Jan. 20, 1975	+ 390	420	$1,260
1975-76	Apr. 19, 1976	− 753	Jan. 30, 1976	0	753	$2,259
1976-77	Jan. 26, 1977	− 60	Nov. 3, 1976	+ 468	528	$1,584
1977-78	Feb. 13, 1978	− 585	Apr. 10, 1978	+ 108	693	$2,079
1978-79	Apr. 11, 1979	− 430	Sept. 12, 1978	− 38	392	$1,176
1979-80	Sept. 21, 1979	+ 133	Apr. 1, 1980	+1022	889	$2,667
1980-81	Oct. 22, 1980	+ 148	Apr. 13, 1981	+1460	1312	$3,936
1981-82	Feb. 3, 1982	+ 18	Dec. 18, 1981	+ 485	467	$1,401
1982-83	Aug. 23, 1982	−1045	Mar. 31, 1983	− 167	878	$2,634
1983-84	Dec. 27, 1983	+ 290	Oct. 10, 1983	+ 862	572	$1,716
1984-85	Sept. 6, 1984	− 237	Oct. 24, 1984	+ 225	462	$1,386

HOGS
L December - S April (same calendar year)

Year	Jan. 24 Initiate Spread at	Mar. 27 Liquidate Spread at	Maximum Adversity	Maximum Profitability	Gain/Loss	Spread Value
1971	+ 425	+ 500	− $ 450	+ $ 225	+ 75	+ $ 225
1972	− 268	+ 153	− $ 21	+ $1,263	+ 421	+ $1,263
1973	− 350	− 150	− $ 696	+ $ 600	+ 200	+ $ 600
1974	+ 18	+ 678	0	+ $3,135	+ 660	+ $1,980
1975	+ 362	+ 310	− $ 876	+ $ 78	− 52	− $ 156
1976	− 90	− 500	− $1,230	+ $ 270	− 410	− $1,230
1977	− 30	+ 160	− $ 90	+ $1,014	+ 190	+ $ 570
1978	− 415	− 187	− $ 510	+ $ 684	+ 228	+ $ 684
1979	− 322	− 260	− $ 204	+ $ 531	+ 62	+ $ 186
1980	+ 470	+ 893	0	+ $1,380	+ 423	+ $1,269
1981	+ 633	+1245	0	+ $1,836	+ 612	+ $1,826
1982	+ 145	+ 410	− $ 381	+ $ 795	+ 265	+ $ 795
1983	− 555	− 170	0	+ $1,155	+ 385	+ $1,155
1984	+ 455	+ 735	− $ 66	+ $ 840	+ 280	+ $ 840
1985	+ 35	+ 120	− $ 81	+ $ 264	+ 85	+ $ 255*

86% Correct in 15 Years

3424 Points Net Profit

$10,272 Net Profit

* Day out February 8, 1985—latest data available

98

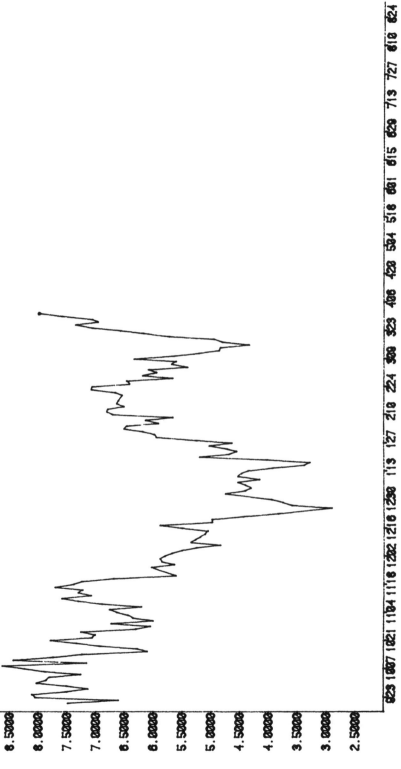

Figure 16
HOGS
(L Dec 84 - S Apr 84)

99

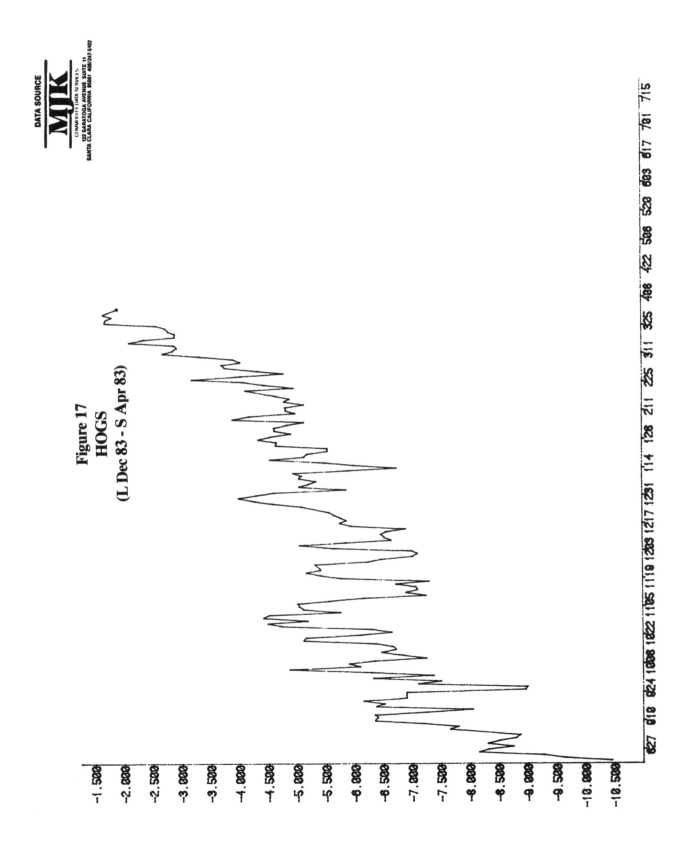

Figure 17
HOGS
(L Dec 83 - S Apr 83)

Chapter 10

Pork Bellies

A by-product of hogs, pork bellies share many of the same supply and demand characteristics of the live animals. The size of the pig crop tends to dictate prices, since the demand for bellies remains relatively inelastic to price changes. Unlike hogs, however, which must be brought to market soon after they reach slaughter weight, pork bellies are frozen and placed in storage where they may remain as long as eight months. Belly traders rely on several key reports to analyze the direction of the market. The "Monthly Cold Storage Reports," which are released about mid-month and analyze the cold-storage holdings as of the first of the month, are eagerly awaited by traders and often have a temporarily violent impact on prices. The monthly storage figures are often anticipated by using daily and weekly storage data, which are generally available from the Chicago Mercantile Exchange. In general, when the hog slaughter is heavy during the fall and winter months, the excess bellies which are not immediately consumed are placed in storage. As slaughter declines, generally from May through September, the movement is then out of storage, and cold-storage stocks decline. The decline in stocks generally culminates during the month of October, when the "spring pig" crop is slaughtered and the stocks again begin to build as excess bellies are moved into storage. An important factor to consider in analyzing belly prices is that supplies are almost always consumed in a given "freeze year." Thus slaughter and consumption will balance out over the course of a year, which begins and ends on October 1. For this reason, the amount of bellies stored, and the changes in stored stocks, become important indicators of price changes.

The key to production figures rests with the hog farrowing data of the previous six-to-eight-month period. Since hogs are normally on feed for at least six months previous to slaughter, the number of farrowings or births six months back can provide a vital clue as to the belly statistics that are about to be announced. Seasonally, hog production reaches a maximum in late fall and early winter—October to December—and falls to a minimum during the months of June, July, and August. As a result of this seasonal pattern, storage stocks tend to increase during the winter and peak during the month of May prior to being drawn down during the summer. While the cold-storage stock statistics can be vitally important during the late winter, spring and summer, be aware that low stocks in the fall are not necessarily bullish, since there are frequently ample supplies of fresh belly production. Thus, look for the storage figure to become important late in the contract year—during May and June—when consumption exceeds production.

Against this background of a highly seasonal ebb and flow in the supply and demand that is relatively inelastic to price, it isn't hard to generalize about the trend of prices. Pork belly prices will generally peak between July and September, when production is at its lowest and stocks are being drawn out of storage at a quickening rate. Conversely, the lows in belly prices occur at a peak (late fall), when there is a heavy movement into storage, ensuring a ready supply.

MAY VS. FEBRUARY PORK BELLIES

If we were permitted only one generalization about this spread it would be that February tends to go off the board weak in terms of its back months. In six of the last seven years, February was weakest in terms of May during the month of February. Given the reliability of February bellies to expire weak relative to May bellies, it's a safe bet to go long May bellies and short February bellies sometime during the previous fall. But when? There tend to be two time periods when the spread appears quite advantageous. The first is during mid-October, when February has usually shown a nice run up from the August-September period over May. And the second occurs in mid-November, when February also tends to be momentarily strong. Aggressive traders should begin by trading the forward spread—long February pork bellies, short May pork bellies—during mid-August and hold the spread until February shows signs of weakening, probably around mid-October. At that time, take the other side by back spreading—long May pork bellies, short February pork bellies—and hold your position into November, when you again take profits. Wait for February to stage its momentary rise, and then again back spread by buying May and selling February and liquidate the spread on February 1st. Less aggressive traders can simply go long May bellies and short February bellies on October 15 and hold the spread into the delivery month (See Table 14 and results, together with Figures 18 and 19).

TRADING RULE

Buy May pork bellies, sell February pork bellies on October 15. Liquidate the spread on February 1.

Table 14
PORK BELLIES
(L May - S February (same calendar year))

	Most negative difference			Most positive difference		
Year	Date	Spread Price Difference	Date	Spread Price Difference	Gain From Low to High	Spread Value
1972-73	Sept. 27, 1972	− 313	Feb. 12, 1973	+ 55	368	$1,324
1973-74	Aug. 6, 1973	− 515	Feb. 21, 1974	+ 195	710	$2,556
1974-75	May 28, 1974	− 47	Feb. 21, 1975	+ 252	299	$1,076
1975-76	Oct. 6, 1975	− 1183	Mar. 26, 1975	+ 100	1283	$4,618
1976-77	Jun. 7, 1976	− 85	Feb. 9, 1977	+ 165	250	$ 900
1977-78	Jan. 11, 1978	− 417	Feb. 21, 1978	+ 123	540	$2,052
1978-79	Sept. 21, 1978	− 257	Feb. 13, 1979	+ 90	347	$1,318
1979-80	May 11, 1979	− 37	Jan. 2, 1980	+ 285	322	$1,223
1980-81	Jul. 16, 1980	+ 20	Dec. 18, 1980	+ 360	340	$1,292
1981-82	Feb. 8, 1982	− 30	May 1, 1981	+ 245	275	$1,045
1982-83	Sept. 10, 1982	− 647	Apr. 6, 1982	+ 155	802	$3,047
1983-84	Feb. 17, 1983	− 122	Feb. 1, 1984	+ 265	387	$1,470

.

PORK BELLIES
L May - S February

Year	Oct. 15 Initiate Spread at	Feb. 1 Liquidate Spread at	Maximum Adversity	Maximum Profitability	Gain/Loss	Spread Value
1972-73	− 265	− 75	− $ 27	+ $ 798	+ 190	+ $ 722
1973-74	− 42	+ 118	− $308	+ $ 680	+ 160	+ $ 608
1974-75	+ 70	+ 98	− $133	+ $ 331	+ 28	+ $ 106
1975-76	− 955	+ 73	0	+ $3,906	+ 1028	+ $3,906
1976-77	+ 33	+ 130	− $220	+ $ 490	+ 97	+ $ 369
1977-78	− 170	− 110	− $939	+ $ 646	+ 60	+ $ 228
1978-79	− 135	− 25	− $ 68	+ $ 798	+ 110	+ $ 418
1979-80	+ 80	+ 268	0	+ $ 779	+ 188	+ $ 714
1980-81	+ 125	+ 290	0	+ $ 893	+ 165	+ $ 627
1981-82	+ 100	+ 212	− $228	+ $ 551	+ 112	+ $ 426
1982-83	− 243	+ 35	− $179	+ $1,056	+ 278	+ $1,056
1983-84	+ 193	+ 265	− $346	+ $ 274	+ 72	+ $ 274
1984-85	+ 97	+ 125	− $312	+ $ 456	+ 28	+ $ 106

100% Correct in 13 Years

2516 Points Net Profit

$9,560 Net Profit

Figure 18
PORK BELLIES
(L May 84 - S Feb 84)

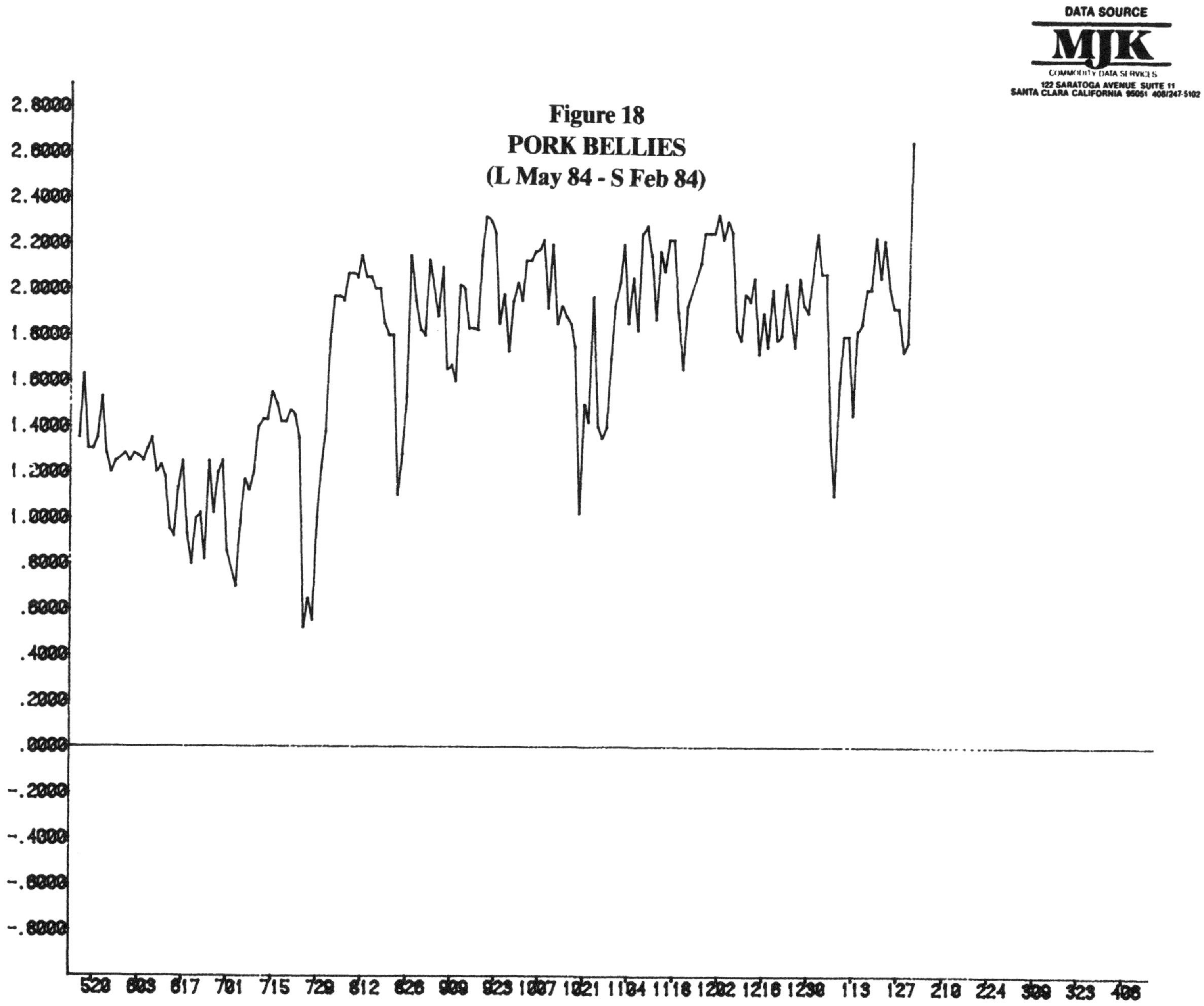

DATA SOURCE

MJK

COMMODITY DATA SERVICES
122 SARATOGA AVENUE SUITE 11
SANTA CLARA CALIFORNIA 95051 408/247-5102

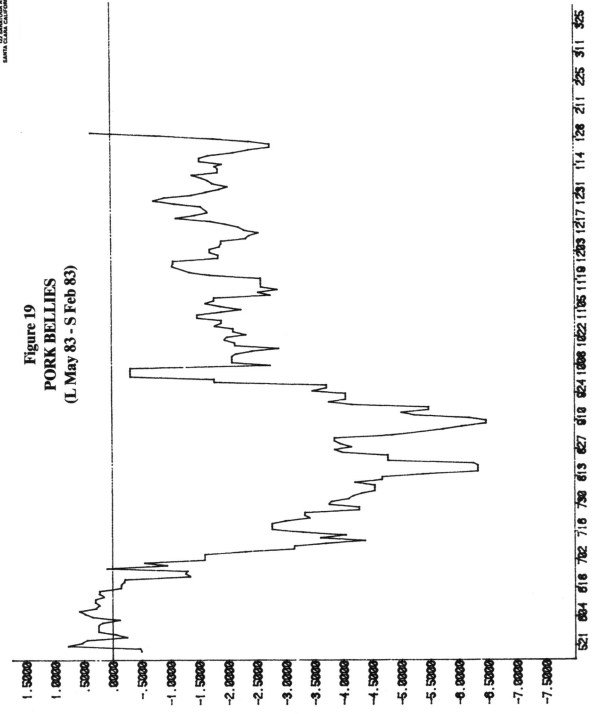

Figure 19
PORK BELLIES
(L May 83 - S Feb 83)

Part III

Interdelivery Food
And Fiber Spreads

Chapter 11

Orange Juice

No other commodity is as dependent on the vagaries of the weather as frozen concentrated orange juice futures. Orange juice becomes a weather market each fall and winter, as bullish speculators eagerly await the first hurricane or freeze. In recent years, freeze scares have been particularly profitable for orange juice traders, usually in the mid-January to mid-February period, although during 1980 the freeze didn't occur until the first week in March. Cold arctic weather sweeping down into Florida orange groves can severely endanger the orange crop which is, of course, the prime source of supply for concentrate. The importance of the weather in Florida cannot be underestimated in attempting to forecast orange juice concentrate futures prices. About one-fourth of the total world supply of oranges is grown in Florida, and approximately three-quarters of all Florida oranges end up as concentrate. While demand for orange juice can vary according to price, the supply of oranges remains the prime force behind orange juice prices. Not only are the orange trees particularly sensitive to weather, but their yields can be greatly influenced by the weather. Thus, even a freeze that doesn't succeed in totally damaging a crop can wreak havoc by harming the yield.

Orange juice prices are subject to sudden, quick moves and are ideal for the risk-oriented speculator—*if* he is willing to admit that the market won't cooperate with him every year. The spread margins are low and the risk is minimal during certain times of the year. But the key factor in whether the trade will work is something over which we have no control—the weather. With over 90 percent of the orange groves in the United States located in Central Florida, the weather in that area remains vitally important. During January, 1977, a devastating frost in Florida resulted in the retail price of orange juice concentrate doubling. For futures speculators, of course, the profit potential was magnified many times over due to the leverage involved.

The key areas of supply for oranges are production, imports, carryover, and cold storage. Imports refer not only to oranges grown in other countries, but oranges which are "imported" into Florida from other orange-producing states outside of Florida, such as California and Texas. The cold storage inventories tend to be lowest at the end of the crop year, during October, November, and December. With the Florida harvest beginning in December and ending in Mid-June, the timing of any weather-related incident, such as a hurricane or a freeze, can also be an important influence on the eventual size of the crop. For instance, a freeze on January 1st, well before the harvest is completed, will tend to have a greater impact on prices than, say, a freeze late in the winter, such as March 15. Year-end carryover of frozen concentrate can also influence prices and should be considered before taking a position.

The recent performance of this orange juice spread suggests that when it works it is worth the risk and when it doesn't work the risk is minimal. In the past five years, the spread has earned approximately 45 percent of the profit it had earned in the previous seven. Given the short-duration that the spread is held, this strategy should be welcome as a potential windfall play should the freeze scare materialize.

NOVEMBER VS. JANUARY ORANGE JUICE

This spread involves going long the November and short the more distant January contract at the beginning of a new calendar year—when the distant January first comes on the boards. Should a freeze scare occur in January or February, the spread will improve as November gains on the January contract. Typically, when the November is run up on a freeze scare, it will retreat prior to the end of the summer and usually go off the boards weak in November, *unless* a hurricane or other weather event destroys the crop in the fall (See Table 15 and results, together with Figures 20 and 21).

TRADING RULE

Buy November orange juice and sell the distant January orange juice futures on January 2. Liquidate the spread on February 22.

Table 15
ORANGE JUICE
L November - S January

	Most negative difference			Most positive difference		
Year	Date	Spread Difference	Date	Spread Price Difference	Gain From Low to High	Spread Value
1972-73	Nov. 16, 1973	−270	Sept. 27, 1972	+ 450	720	$ 1,080
1973-74	May 9, 1974	−350	Feb. 7, 1974	+ 180	530	$ 795
1974-75	Nov. 14, 1975	−270	Mar. 17, 1975	− 100	170	$ 255
1975-76	Sept. 24, 1976	−165	Nov. 12, 1976	+ 150	315	$ 472
1976-77	Dec. 23, 1976	−140	Nov. 16, 1977	+6725	6865	$10,297
1977-78	Nov. 16, 1978	−350	Feb. 22, 1978	+2075	2425	$ 3,637
1978-79	Sept. 10, 1979	− 80	Nov.16, 1979	+1440	1550	$ 2,325
1979-80	Oct. 13, 1980	−350	Jan. 31, 1980	+ 130	480	$ 720
1980-81	Aug. 21, 1981	−505	Mar. 3, 1981	+ 420	925	$ 1,387
1981-82	Jun. 3, 1982	−270	Nov. 15, 1982	+ 220	490	$ 735
1982-83	Jan. 20, 1983	−100	Nov. 15, 1983	+1210	1310	$ 1,965
1983-84	Oct. 31, 1984	−410	Nov. 29, 1983	+ 580	990	$ 1,485

ORANGE JUICE
L November - S January

Year	Jan. 2 Initiate Spread at	Feb. 22 Liquidate Spread at	Maximum Adversity	Maximum Profitability	Gain/Loss	Spread Value
1973	+ 100	− 20	− $240	+ $ 135	− 80	− $ 120
1974	+ 30	+ 90	0	+ $ 225	+ 60	+ $ 90
1975	− 150	− 110	0	+ $ 75	+ 40	+ $ 60
1976	− 80	− 80	− $ 22	+ $ 15	0	0
1977	− 100	+ 200	− $ 45	+ $ 833	+300	+ $ 450
1978	+1325	+2075	− $840	+ $1,125	+750	+ $1,125
1979	+ 600	+ 285	− $472	+ $ 307	−315	− $ 472
1980	+ 35	0	− $128	+ $ 142	− 35	− $ 53
1981	− 75	+ 320	− $ 82	+ $ 742	+395	+ $ 593
1982	− 50	− 110	− $195	+ $ 83	− 60	− $ 90
1983	− 50	+ 100	− $ 75	+ $ 255	+150	+ $ 225
1984	+ 470	+ 365	− $593	+ $ 82	−105	− $ 158

50% Correct in 12 Years
1100 Points Net Profit
$1,650 Net Profit

111

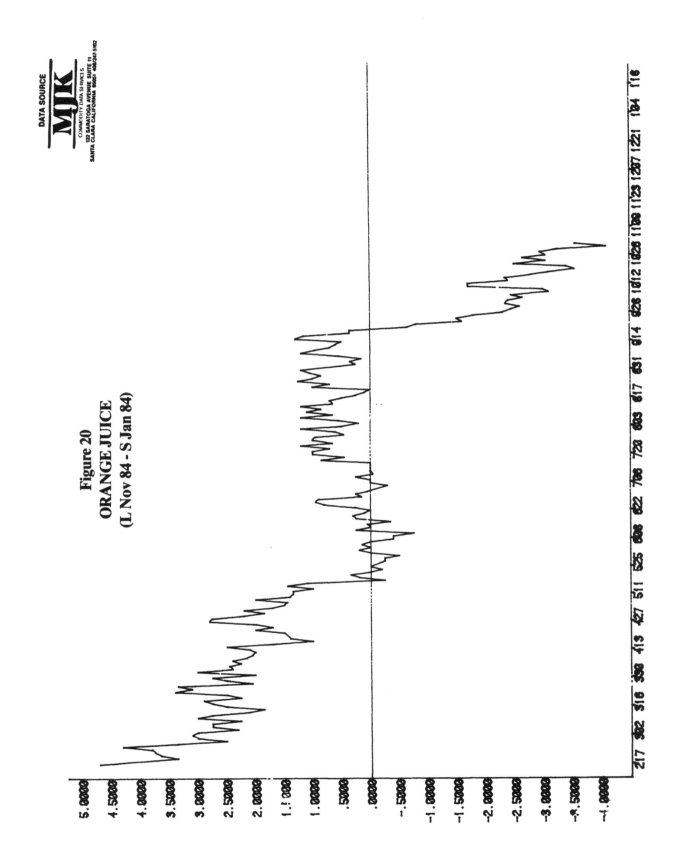

Figure 20
ORANGE JUICE
(L Nov 84 - S Jan 84)

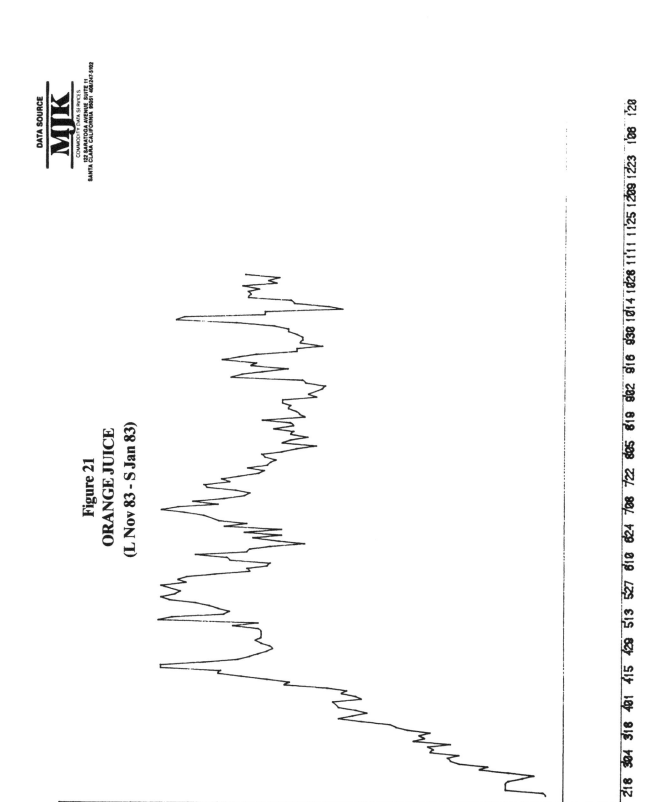

Figure 21
ORANGE JUICE
(L Nov 83 - S Jan 83)

113

Chapter 12

World Sugar

Most of the sugar produced in the free world is bought and sold under contractual agreements that limit price fluctuations. The remainder of the available sugar, however, which is known as "unprotected" or "free" sugar, is allowed to fluctuate freely and is priced according to strict supply and demand. According to different sources, the so-called free sugar accounts for as little as 8 percent to as much as one-third of the sugar produced each year. Because this unprotected sugar is just a small part of the total production, relatively small changes in the total sugar production outlook can translate into significant price moves on the New York and London sugar exchanges.

In recent years, sugar has been a lackluster performer, remaining relatively stable. But the 1979-80 market was highlighted by skyrocketing prices, suggesting that stable sugar prices can be deceptive. As a rule, every five or six years the sugar market booms following a period of dormant prices.

The spread trader should pay particular attention to the intercrop sugar spreads, such as those in May-October and March-October sugar. The signal to look for is a decline in sugar stocks in the September 1 report, which is the beginning of the new marketing year. In the past, most bull moves in sugar have been signalled by this decline in stocks at the beginning of the new crop year.

MAY VS. SEPTEMBER SUGAR

The seasonal move in this spread tends to begin during mid-September and carries into mid-January. The spread trader should note that we are referring here to an intercrop spread of two contract months of the *same* calendar year. Thus, in the fall of 1985, you should be spread long May 1986 sugar against short September 1986 sugar. During 1986, of course, you will spread the 1987 contracts—and so on. Although not the most reliable spread, this trade can be quite profitable in those years when sugar makes a significant bull move. In the absence of the bull move, the spread is apt to just meander sideways, as it did during 1975, 1977, and 1978, and every year since 1980. The spread tends to peak in the November-January period and then drifts more negative. Although the spread took a precipitous drop in March 1980 our rule would have safely had you out of the market at that time. For reliability, trade the spread during the fall months when its record of consistency is the best (See Table 16 and results, together with Figures 22 and 23).

TRADING RULE

Buy May sugar and sell the distant September sugar on September 15. Liquidate the spread on January 15.

Table 16
SUGAR
L May - S September

Year	Most negative difference			Most positive difference		
	Date	Spread Sprice Difference	Date	Spread Price Difference	Gain From Low to High	Spread Value
1972-73	Sept. 14, 1972	+ 6	Jan. 12, 1973	+ 148	142	$1,590
1973-74	Aug. 13, 1973	+ 16	Mar. 22, 1974	+ 576	560	$6,272
1974-75	Apr. 30, 1975	+ 73	Dec. 4, 1974	+ 739	666	$7,459
1975-76	Apr. 28, 1976	− 31	Apr. 21, 1975	+ 189	220	$2,464
1976-77	Dec. 28, 1976	− 61	Jul. 6,. 1976	+ 81	142	$1,590
1977-78	Oct. 17, 1977	− 71	Apr. 5, 1977	+ 10	81	$ 907
1978-79	Apr. 27, 1979	−100	Oct. 25, 1978	− 21	79	$ 884
1979-80	Mar. 10, 1980	−577	Nov. 30, 1979	+ 42	619	$6,932
1980-81	Apr. 29, 1981	−186	Oct. 20, 1980	+481	667	$7,470
1981-82	Apr. 19, 1982	− 77	Apr. 30, 1982	− 1	76	$ 851
1982-83	Apr. 13, 1983	− 86	Jun. 2, 1982	− 28	58	$ 649
1983-84	Apr. 25, 1984	−105	Jun. 1, 1983	− 23	82	$ 918
1984-85	May 3, 1984	− 79	Oct. 24, 1984	− 46	33	$ 369

SUGAR
L May - S September

Year	Sept. 15 Initiate Spread at	Jan. 15 Liquidate Spread at	Maximum Adversity	Maximum Profitability	Gain/Loss	Spread Value
1972-73	+ 13	+ 146	− $ 56	+ $1,512	+ 133	+ $1,490
1973-74	+ 44	+ 148	− $ 123	+ $1,310	+ 104	+ $1,165
1974-75	+ 369	+ 447	− $ 918	+ $4,144	+ 78	+ $ 874
1975-76	+ 26	+ 2	− $ 470	0	− 24	− $ 269
1976-77	− 41	− 6	− $ 224	+ $ 482	+ 35	+ $ 392
1977-78	− 42	− 44	− $ 325	+ $ 101	− 2	− $ 22
1978-79	− 40	− 45	− $ 146	+ $ 213	− 5	− $ 56
1979-80	− 53	− 8	− $ 157	+ $1,064	+ 45	+ $ 504
1980-81	+ 193	+ 23	− $1,904	+ $3,226	− 170	− $1,904
1981-82	− 37	− 34	− $ 291	+ $ 134	+ 3	+ $ 34
1982-83	− 63	− 68	− $ 123	+ $ 246	− 5	− $ 56
1983-84	− 52	− 58	− $ 134	+ $ 134	− 6	− $ 67
1984-85	− 58	− 60	− $ 134	+ $ 134	− 2	− $ 22

46% Correct in 13 Years
174 Points Net Profit
$1,949 Net Profit

Figure 22
SUGAR
(L May 84 - S Sep 84)

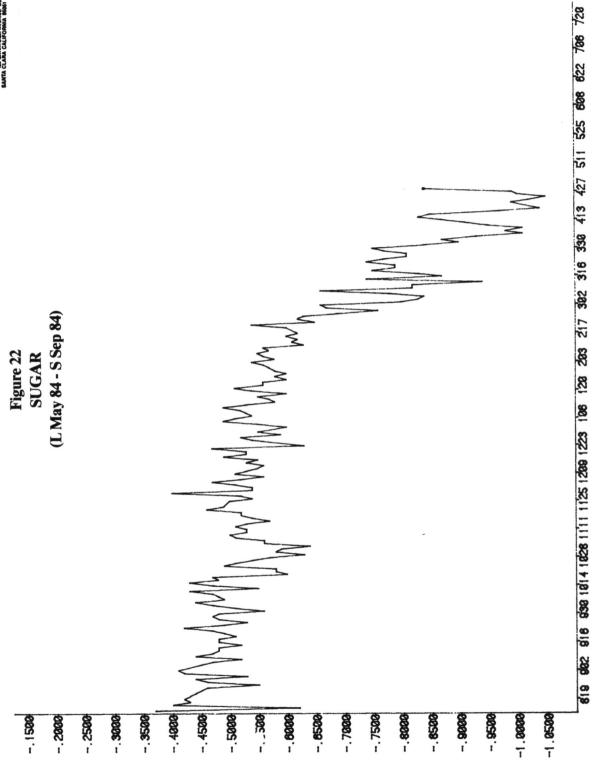

118

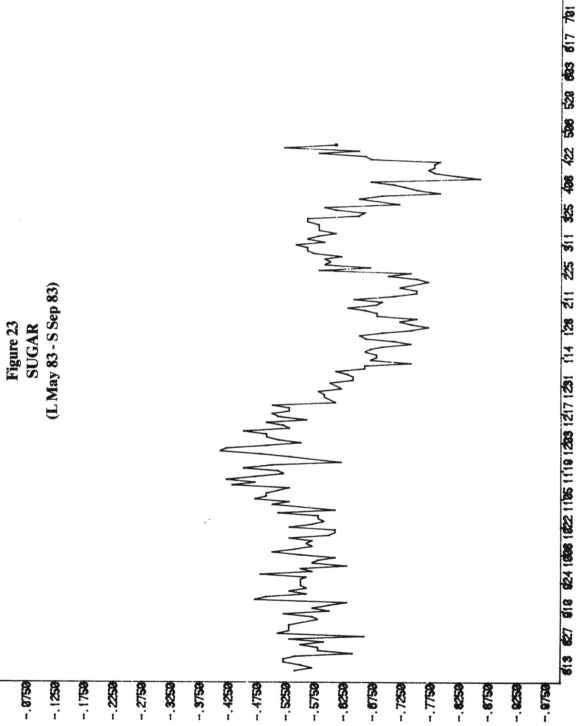

Figure 23
SUGAR
(L May 83 - S Sep 83)

119

Chapter 13

Cocoa

The cocoa crop year, which runs from October through the following September, tends to be characterized by periods when prices rise and fall on a fairly predictable pattern. Cocoa is harvested in two main periods during the crop year with the first period, which runs from October through March, accounting for 80 percent of the crop. A second mid-crop is harvested later in the year—normally in May and June—and yields the other 20 percent of cocoa production. Cocoa price moves are characterized by long, sustained uptrends and downtrends that are a technical analyst's dream since they rarely violate trendlines, except on a major price reversal. This, it should be added, is in sharp contrast to a number of other commodities that reveal no rhyme or reason in their price movements.

The size of the cocoa crop is always a mystery every year, since the stocks are divided into so-called "visible" stocks and "invisible" stocks. With much of the production concentrated in Ghana and other West African nations, the best estimates are often far from accurate. The "visible" stocks consist of stocks on hand in licensed warehouses. The "invisible" stocks, however, which consist of supplies in unlicensed, or private, warehouses are not made public and the abundance or scarcity of these stocks can be the undoing of many a good fundamental analysis. Since cocoa is a "world" commodity, there is no central U.S. agency, such as the USDA, that releases accurate figures on the relevant crop statistics. Moreover, the crop is subject to devastation when a sudden drought occurs and a formerly promising cocoa crop is wiped out almost overnight. Since it takes four years before a cocoa tree will bear fruit, the crop may be affected for a number of years by a single aberration in the weather. Despite the new crop's size, knowledge of a surplus or tight supplies is not enough. The cocoa analyst must also take into account the size of the carryover, which is another important supply variable.

Demand for cocoa is mostly a function of income. Since the cocoa beans are used to manufacture candy, the end product is consumed primarily in those Western countries that have acquired a taste for chocolate, primarily the Western European countries and the United States. In recent years, the speculative activity in cocoa has lagged, while speculators have participated heavily in trading domestic agricultural commodities. The speculative boom in the winter of 1980, however was in part due to traders switching to cocoa after having had a good run in the sugar market. Understandably, the boom disappeared as quickly as it originally occurred, and cocoa prices took a plunge after having been bid up to unrealistic levels on no fundamental news.

In general, cocoa remains very much a hedger's commodity and would-be cocoa speculators must recognize this. On the one hand, this is a very positive feature of the market, since it means the seasonal patterns are quite intact as hedgers place and lift their positions. On the other, it means the astute speculator must be aware of what side of the market he is on and not try to "fade" the commercials who, after all, are intimately acquainted with the supply and demand situation.

SEPTEMBER VS. MAY COCOA

This spread has an uneven trading history and works only about 50 percent of the time. The basic strategy is to look for a summer rally in cocoa to push the nearer May contract up over the September and then back spread in the fall in anticipation of a falling back into line of the two months. Please note that we are referring here to the spread in cocoa a year out. Thus the long 1981 September cocoa would be spread against the nearer short 1981 May cocoa during the month of September in 1980. The spread is apt to work best, of course, following a summer rally, which typically occurs during late July or early August. Unfortunately, like many seasonal spreads, this one doesn't work every year (See Table 17 and results, together with Figures 24 and 25).

TRADING RULES

Buy the distant September cocoa one year out and sell the nearer May cocoa on September 1. Liquidate the spread on November 30. To take advantage of the annual summer rally in cocoa prices, buy May cocoa and sell September cocoa for maturity one year out on June 1. Liquidate the spread on July 15.

Table 17
Cocoa
L September - S May

	Most negative difference			Most positive difference		
Year	Date	Spread Price Difference	Date	Spread Price Difference	Gain From Low to High	Spread Value
1972-73	May 16, 1973	− 570	Aug. 22, 1972	+ 60	630	$1,890
1973-74	Apr. 4, 1974	− 1570	May 29, 1973	+ 45	1615	$4,845
1974-75	Nov. 8, 1974	− 770	May 21, 1974	− 165	605	$1,815
1975-76	May 7, 1976	− 1030	Jul. 1, 1975	+ 50	1080	$3,240
1976-77	Apr. 27, 1977	− 1350	Apr. 12, 1976	− 195	1155	$3,465
1977-78	Jul. 20, 1977	− 1370	Feb. 21, 1978	− 455	915	$2,745
1978-79	Nov. 28, 1978	− 550	Feb. 21, 1979	+ 655	1205	$3,615
1979-80	Data Not Available Due to Change in Contract Size					
1980-81	Dec. 29, 1980	+ 70	Apr. 30, 1981	+ 139	69	$ 690
1981-82	May 5, 1981	− 22	Jun. 18, 1981	+ 120	142	$1,420
1982-83	Jan. 25, 1983	− 1	Oct. 5, 1982	+ 90	91	$ 910
1983-84	Feb. 2, 1984	− 75	Apr. 13, 1984	+ 61	136	$1,360
1984-85	Jan. 28, 1985	− 62	Jul. 6, 1984	+ 53	115	$1,150

COCOA
L September - S May

Year	Sept. 1 Initiate Spread at	Nov. 30 Liquidate Spread at	Maximum Adversity	Maximum Profitability	Gain/Loss	Spread Value
1972	+ 46	+ 35	− $ 93	+ $ 36	− 11	− $ 33
1973	− 195	− 105	− $ 390	+ $ 420	+ 90	+ $ 270
1974	− 635	− 465	− $ 405	+ $ 510	+ 170	− $ 195
1975	− 135	− 200	− $ 555	+ $ 195	− 65	− $ 540
1976	− 725	− 905	− $1,110	+ $ 60	− 180	− $ 195
1977	− 1045	− 610	− $ 765	+ $1,335	+ 435	+ $1,305
1978	− 475	− 500	− $ 225	+ $1,065	− 25	− $ 75
1979	+ 290	+ 335	− $ 15	+ $ 930	+ 45	+ $ 135
1980	+ 103	+ 99	− $ 330	0	− 4	− $ 40*
1981	+ 54	+ 50	− $ 250	+ $ 280	− 4	− $ 40
1982	+ 77	+ 68	− $ 100	− $ 130	− 9	− $ 90
1983	+ 40	+ 16	− $ 300	+ $ 170	− 24	− $ 240
1984	+ 34	+ 12	− $ 430	0	− 22	− $ 220

31% Correct in 13 Years
$747 Net Profit**

* Reflects new 10 metric ton contract
** Points Net Profit not applicable due to change in contract size

COCOA
L May - S September

Year	June 1 Initiate Spread at	July 15 Liquidate Spread at	Maximum Adversity	Maximum Profitability	Gain/Loss	Spread Value
1973	− 40	+ 265	0	+ $915	+ 305	+ $915
1974	+ 180	+ 455	0	+ $840	+ 275	+ $825
1975	− 50	− 25	0	+ $108	+ 25	+ $ 75
1976	+ 453	+ 525	− $ 54	+ $396	+ 72	+ $216
1977	+ 1125	+ 1280	− $390	+ $600	+ 155	+ $465
1978*	+ 280	+ 370	0	+ $615	+ 60	+ $270
—						
1982	− 100	− 57	− $200	+ $430	+ 43	+ $430**
1983	− 76	− 79	− $ 30	0	− 3	− $ 30
1984	− 35	− 26	0	+ $290	+ 9	+ $ 90
1985	− 42	− 20	− $110	+ $220	+ 22	+ $220

90% Correct in 10 Years
$3,476 Net Profit***

---

*   Data between 1978 and 1982 not available
**   Reflects new 10 metric ton contract
*** Points Net Profit not applicable due to change in contract size

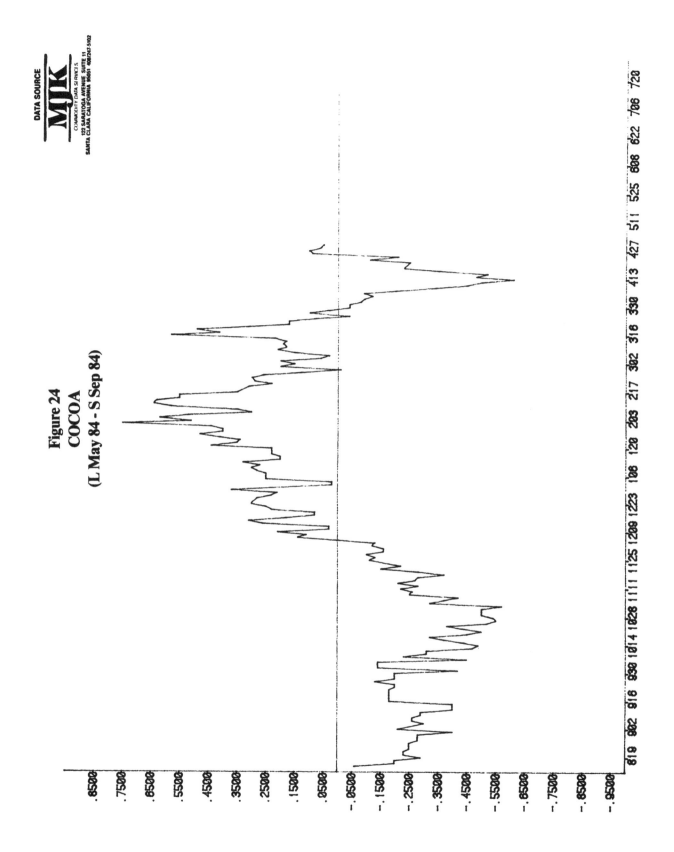

Figure 24
COCOA
(L May 84 - S Sep 84)

125

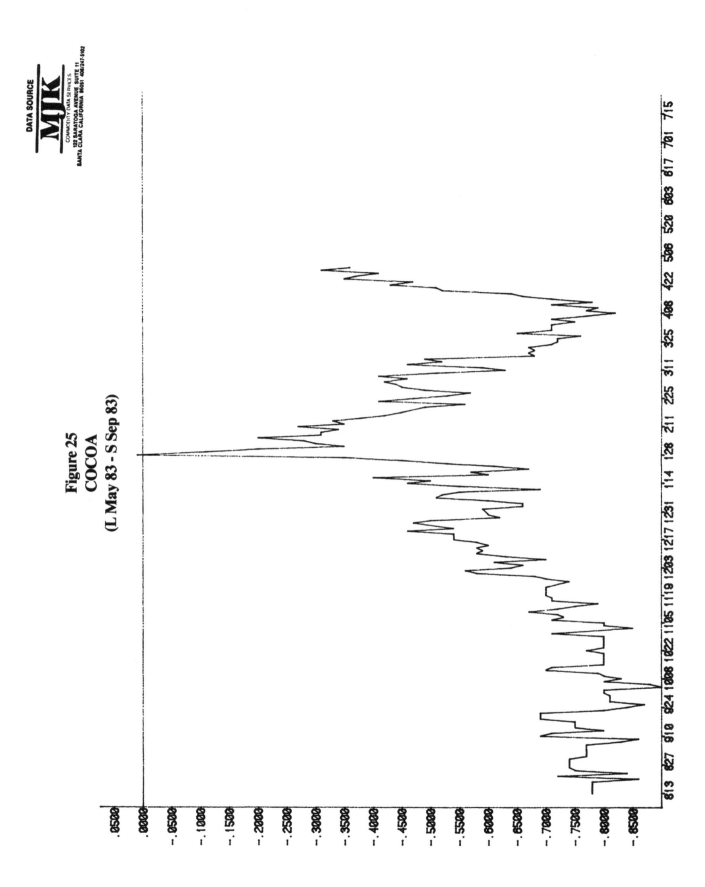

Figure 25
COCOA
(L May 83 - S Sep 83)

Chapter 14

Cotton

Like a number of other agricultural commodities, cotton has a fairly reliable seasonal pattern based upon predictable changes in supply that occur during and after the harvest period. The cotton crop year runs from August 1 through July 31, with the harvest taking place from September through December. The fundamental situation is complex because so many variables have to be taken into account in analyzing the market. But a number of key factors stand out. Since the 1930's, the U.S. government has played an important role in the cotton supply and demand situation—and an analysis of the market must include the impact of the latest government programs. In recent years, the introduction of synthetic fibers has had a depressing impact on cotton prices, as users have turned toward the competing fibers. But the sharp boost in petroleum prices has resulted in an increase in the use of natural cotton, since the synthetic products require petroleum in their manufacture.

Grown primarily in the Sun Belt, an area ranging from the Deep South westward to California, cotton is highly sensitive to weather conditions. During the harvest period, it often pays to keep a close watch on weather reports and monitor the USDA cotton production forecasts, which are released on a regular basis.

Seasonally, cotton, like a number of other agricultural commodities, tends to reach its lows during and immediately after the harvest. It then rises to its highs later in the season.

Cotton

DECEMBER VS. JULY COTTON

The reliability factor for the short July cotton to go off the boards weak is rather high. In six out of the past seven years, the most positive move in this spread was registered between May 28 and July 9. The ideal initiation period is not quite clearcut, but it is preferable to wait until after the harvest for entry. February 15 is used as the entry date in the results below (See Table 18 and results, together with Figures 26 and 27).

TRADING RULE

Buy December cotton and sell July cotton on February 15. Liquidate the spread on June 30.

Table 18
COTTON
L December - S July (same calendar year)

	Most negative difference			Most positive difference		
Year	Date	Spread Price Difference	Date	Spread Price Difference	Gain From Low to High	Spread Value
1972-73	Apr. 12, 1973	− 721	Jul. 6, 1973	+ 260	981	$4,905
1973-74	Sept. 6, 1973	− 2065	May 28, 1974	− 323	1742	$8,710
1974-75	Jul. 30, 1974	− 120	Jan. 23, 1975	+ 335	455	$2,275
1975-76	Jun. 24, 1976	− 555	Jul. 1, 1975	+ 115	670	$3,350
1976-77	Oct. 29, 1976	− 1417	Jul. 7, 1977	− 68	1349	$6,745
1977-78	Jul. 5, 1977	− 160	Jul. 7, 1978	+ 492	652	$3,260
1978-79	Nov. 27, 1978	− 824	Jul. 9, 1979	+ 251	1075	$5,375
1979-80	Feb. 5, 1980	− 1068	Oct. 18, 1979	+ 170	1238	$6,190
1980-81	Sept. 12, 1980	− 1197	Jul. 9, 1981	− 115	1082	$5,410
1981-82	Jul. 6, 1981	− 330	Jul. 7, 1982	+ 599	929	$4,645
1982-83	Mar. 29, 1983	− 287	May 25, 1983	+ 281	568	$2,840
1983-84	Nov. 10, 1983	− 826	Jul. 2, 1984	− 256	570	$2,850
1984-85	Jul. 9, 1984	− 260	Sept. 17, 1984	+ 120	380	$1,900

COTTON
L December - S July (same calendar year)

Year	Feb. 15 Initiate Spread at	Jun. 30 Liquidate Spread at	Maximum Adversity	Maximum Profitability	Gain/Loss	Spread Value
1973	− 362	− 67	− $1,795	+ $1,810	+ 295	+ $1,475
1974	− 765	− 704	− $1,225	+ $2,210	+ 61	+ $ 305
1975	+ 290	+ 214	− $ 600	+ $ 55	− 76	− $ 380
1976	− 287	− 293	− $1,340	+ $1,495	− 6	− $ 30
1977	− 739	− 565	− $1,295	+ $3,335	+ 174	+ $ 870
1978	+ 144	+ 447	− $ 70	+ $1,560	+ 303	+ $1,515
1979	− 385	+ 166	0	+ $3,050	+ 551	+ $2,755
1980	− 913	− 617	− $ 310	+ $3,900	+ 296	+ $1,480
1981	− 665	− 671	− $1,230	+ $1,975	− 6	− $ 30
1982	+ 392	+ 495	− $ 280	+ $ 880	+ 103	+ $ 515
1983	− 96	+ 106	− $ 955	+ $1,885	+ 202	+ $1,010
1984	− 306	− 256	− $2,545	+ $ 250	+ 50	+ $ 250

75% Correct in 12 Years

1947 Points Net Profit

$9,735 Net Profit

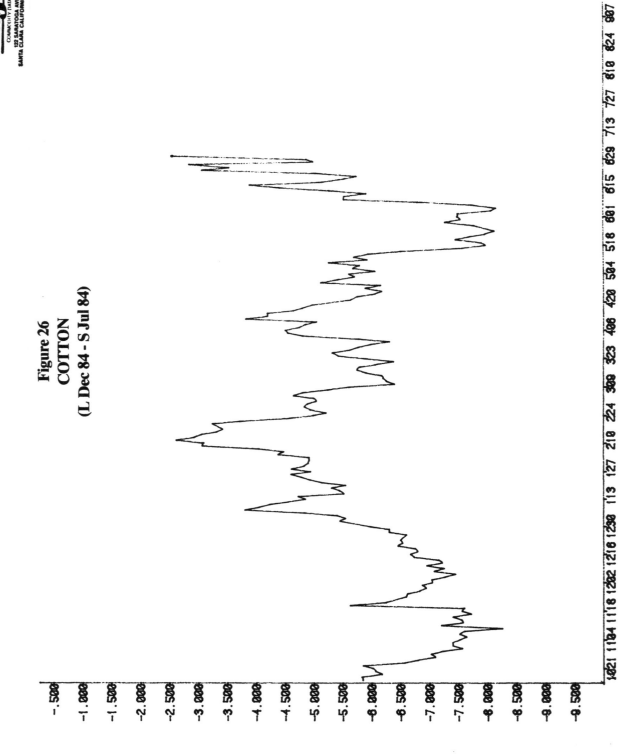

Figure 26
COTTON
(L Dec 84 - S Jul 84)

130

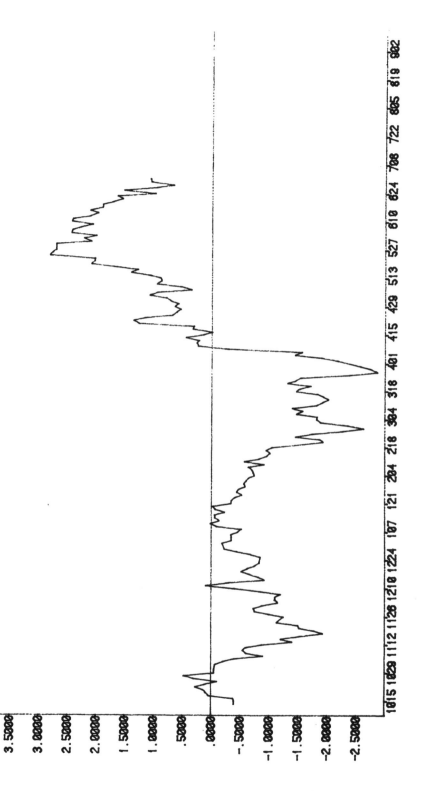

Figure 27
COTTON
(L Dec 83 - S Jul 83)

Part IV
Interdelivery Wood Spreads

Chapter 15

Lumber

Lumber exhibits a strong tendency to reflect the relative health of the housing industry. While there are a number of seasonal relationships in the lumber market, the strongest is the annual summer rally, which can be taken advantage of by bull spreading in the spring months. Since the contra-seasonal pattern occurs almost as frequently as the seasonal pattern in lumber, traders must use caution in placing their spread positions. During the mid-seventies, the contra-seasonal pattern occurred for three consecutive years—from 1975 through 1977—and then reverted to the normal seasonal pattern.

Fundamentalists in the lumber market pay close attention to government housing start statistics. Specifically, the three key indicators are: seasonally-adjusted rates of housing starts, monthly total number of starts, and monthly building permit numbers. Inventory reports and monthly mill production figures also provide an insight into the direction of the market.

Since we now live in an era of high interest rates, the availability of money is perhaps the most crucial determinant of the housing industry—and hence lumber prices.

JULY VS. NOVEMBER LUMBER

As a rule, dealer buying in the lumber market in early spring results in a temporary bulge in prices as the nearer July contract gains on the back months. Please note that the contra-seasonal pattern has occurred almost as frequently as the seasonal pattern in recent years. This lack of consistency makes the trade somewhat higher in risk than other spreads listed in this book (See Table 20 and results, together with Figures 28 and 29).

TRADING RULE

Buy July lumber and sell November lumber on April 1. Liquidate the spread on July 7.

Table 19
LUMBER
L July - S November

| | | Most negative difference | | Most positive difference | | |
Year	Date	Spread Price Difference	Date	Spread Price Difference	Gain From Low to High	Spread Value
1973-74	Feb. 12, 1974	− 250	July 10, 1974	+ 1600	1850	$1,850
1974-75	Jul. 15, 1975	− 2270	May 1, 1975	+ 1120	3390	$3,390
1975-76	May 24, 1976	− 1450	Feb. 20, 1976	+ 470	1920	$1,920
1976-77	Jul. 18, 1977	− 920	Feb. 18, 1977	+ 840	1760	$1,760
1977-78	Dec. 5, 1977	+ 240	Jul. 14, 1978	+ 4170	3930	$3,930
1978-79	Dec. 5, 1978	+ 690	Jul. 5, 1979	+ 3480	2790	$2,790
1979-80	Jul. 7, 1980	− 2430	Jan. 23, 1980	+ 1020	3450	$3,450
1980-81	Mar. 16, 1981	− 1730	Apr. 27, 1981	+ 80	1810	$1,810
1981-82	May 13, 1982	− 1560	Jun. 18, 1982	+ 470	2030	$2,030
1982-83	Jul. 15, 1983	− 1380	May 31, 1983	+ 2150	3530	$3,530
1983-84	Jul. 12, 1984	− 2050	Mar. 19, 1984	+ 340	2390	$2,390
1984-85	Jan. 21, 1985*	− 860	Nov. 7, 1984	0	860	$ 860

* Through February 8, 1985—most recent data available

LUMBER
L July - S November

Year	Apr. 1 Initiate Spread at	Jul. 7 Liquidate Spread at	Maximum Adversity	Maximum Profitability	Gain/Loss	Spread Value
1974	+ 310	+ 1560	− $ 140	+ $1,250	+ 1250	+ $1,250
1975	+ 160	− 1310	− $1,470	+ $ 960	− 1470	− $1,470
1976	+ 40	− 230	− $1,490	+ $ 110	− 270	− $ 270
1977	− 160	− 160	− $ 760	+ $ 40	0	0
1978	+ 1400	+ 2700	− $ 130	+ $1,380	+ 1300	+ $1,300
1979	+ 1070	+ 3090	− $ 90	+ $2,410	+ 2020	+ $2,020
1980	− 210	− 2430	− $2,880	0	− 2220	− $2,220
1981	− 1550	− 980	− $ 220	+ $2,120	− 570	− $ 570
1982	− 830	+ 120	− $ 950	+ $1,690	+ 950	+ $ 950
1983	− 1120	+ 230	− $ 91	+ $4,250	+ 1350	+ $1,350
1984	− 290	− 1810	− $1,990	+ $ 700	− 1520	− $1,520

45% Correct in 11 Years
1820 Points Net Profit
$1,820 Net Profit

Figure 28
LUMBER
(L Nov 84 - S Jul 84)

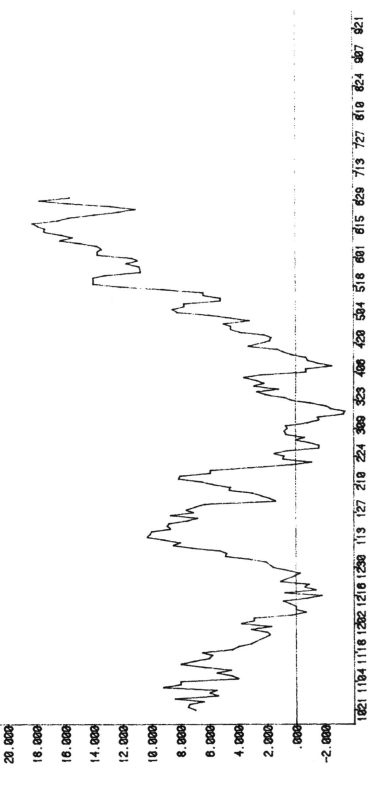

138

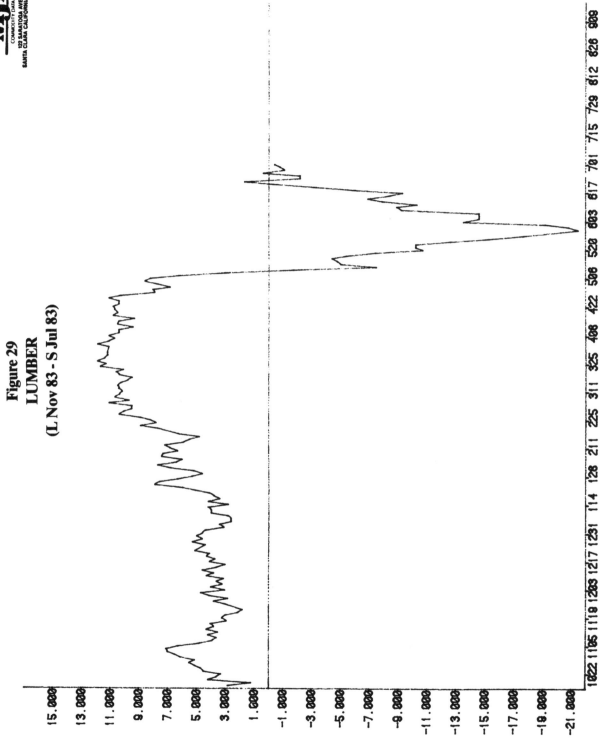

Figure 29
LUMBER
(L Nov 83 - S Jul 83)

139

Part V
Interdelivery Metal Spreads

Chapter 16

Silver

While it would be inaccurate to suggest that silver has a seasonal tendency to rise or fall, as a spread trading vehicle, silver offers many profitable opportunities. Moreover, since the recent surge in metal prices began, the opportunities have become greater and greater as traders, seeking protection from the huge volatility in the metals, have turned increasingly toward spreads.

As a completely storable commodity, silver tends to adhere to the inverse of the General Rule in its price relationships. Specifically, the inverse of the General Rule can be stated as follows: in bull markets, the back months will gain ground on the near months; in bear markets, the near months will gain ground on the back months. Thus, buy the distant month and sell the nearby to take advantage of a bull market; and, buy the nearby and sell the distant month to take advantage of a bear market.

This strategy works because carrying charges will narrow if the market declines, resulting in the distant month falling faster than the nearby; conversely, in a bull market, the carrying charges—whose prime determinant is interest rates—will tend to increase, resulting in the back months, which must be stored and financed longer, gaining ground on the nearbys. There is an exception to this rule, however, with which every speculator must be familiar. This exception occurs when a short squeeze develops. In such a situation, the nearby can be expected to rise faster than the distant months. In a squeeze, the fear develops of there being too little product available to meet delivery. Thus, the hapless shorts must buy back their positions at ever-increasing higher prices, resulting in the limit-less nearby delivery month soaring in relation to the other months. Such a situation can be disastrous for even the most well-financed trader (See Table 20).

TRADING RULE

In a bull market, buy a back month and sell a nearby futures contract. In a bear market, buy a near month and sell a distant month. (Note: since silver does not display seasonal tendencies, more specific instructions cannot be included in this rule).

Table 20

SILVER

L May - S July

| | Most negative difference | | | Most positive difference | | |
Year	Date	Spread Price Difference	Date	Spread Price Difference	Gain From Low to High	Spread Value
1972-73	Mar. 6, 1973	− 400	Jul. 31, 1972	0	400	$ 200
1973-74	May 28, 1974	− 2550	Jun. 18, 1973	0	2,550	$1,275
1974-75	Apr. 25, 1975	− 1570	Mar. 14, 1974	− 300	1,270	$ 635
1975-76	Aug. 22, 1975	− 850	May 25, 1976	− 220	630	$ 315
1976-77	May 26, 1976	− 650	May 25, 1977	− 230	420	$ 210
1977-78	Mar. 31, 1978	− 800	May 25, 1978	− 350	450	$ 225
1978-79	May 8, 1979	− 1750	May 21, 1979	− 400	1,350	$ 674
1979-80	Feb. 29, 1980	− 7500	May 27, 1980	+ 9500	17,000	$8,500
1980-81	Oct. 8, 1980	− 6300	Oct. 16, 1980	+ 1800	8,100	$4,050
1981-82	Sept. 29, 1980	− 6150	May 25,. 1982	− 860	5,290	$2,645
1982-83	Sept. 25, 1981	− 2800	May 25, 1983	− 1100	1,700	$ 850
1983-84	Aug. 17, 1983	− 2400	May 25, 1984	− 900	1,500	$ 750

Chapter 17

Gold

The spread strategy suggested for silver applies equally for gold. Considering the enormous volatility in the metals markets, spreading offers a lower-risk alternative—one that enables you to participate in the profitable opportunities at lower risk. During the last several months of 1979, a single spread in gold, held into the early months of 1980, would have returned enormous profits (See Table 21).

TRADING RULE

In a bull market, buy a distant contract of gold and sell a nearer contract. In a bear market, buy a nearby contract and sell a distant contract. (Note: Here, again, there are no seasonal price moves. Rely on fundamental and technical analysis of the market to determine whether to place bull or bear spreads).

Table 21
COMEX GOLD
L December - S April

	Most negative difference			Most positive difference		
Year	Date	Spread Price Difference	Date	Spread Price Difference	Gain From Low to High	Spread Value
1974-75	Aug. 5, 1975	− 720	Dec. 24, 1975	− 170	550	$ 550
1975-76	Dec. 29, 1975	− 370	Oct. 11, 1976	− 10	360	$ 360
1976-77	Nov. 4, 1977	− 460	Aug. 15, 1977	− 260	200	$ 200
1977-78	Oct. 30, 1978	− 860	Oct. 6, 1977	− 330	530	$ 560
1978-79	Dec. 18, 1979	− 2350	Jun. 8, 1978	− 590	1760	$1,760
1979-80	Mar. 6, 1980	− 5000	Jun. 29, 1979	− 860	4140	$4,140
1980-81	Sept. 23, 1980	− 4120	Dec. 28, 1981	− 1170	2950	$2,950
1981-82	Sept. 10, 1981	− 2800	Dec. 23, 1982	− 1050	1750	$1,750
1982-83	Sept. 9, 1982	− 2170	Dec. 21, 1983	− 930	1240	$1,240
1983-84	Jul. 18, 1983	− 1810	Dec. 26, 1984	− 630	1180	$1,180

Chapter 18

Copper

As with the precious metals, copper spreads adhere to the inverse of the General Rule. Until recently, however, the spread relationships in copper had not gotten out of line. But the big 1979-80 bull market in copper changed all that. During the last weeks of 1979, for instance, a September-March copper spread moved well over 500 points, as the back September contract increased in value at a faster rate than the nearer March 1980 contract.

JULY VS. DECEMBER COPPER

In looking over the table of statistics, you'll see that this spread in copper works only about half the time, alternating each year with the bull copper spread. When it does work, the spread should be initiated on December 1 and held through the first day of the nearer July maturity month. Seasonally, copper prices tend to decline into the summer months. This spread serves to capitalize on that tendency (See Table 22 and results, together with Figures 30 and 31).

TRADING RULE

Buy July copper and sell December copper on December 1. Liquidate the spread on July 1.

Table 22
COPPER
L July - S December

	Most negative difference			**Most positive difference**		
Year	**Date**	**Spread Price Difference**	**Date**	**Spread Price Difference**	**Gain From Low to High**	**Spread Value**
1972-73	Dec. 21, 1972	− 220	Jul. 2, 1973	+ 600	820	$2,050
1973-74	Jul. 5, 1974	− 270	Mar. 29, 1974	+ 1000	1270	$3,175
1974-75	Nov. 8, 1974	− 340	Dec. 6, 1974	− 200	140	$ 350
1975-76	Jun. 24, 1976	− 310	Apr. 8, 1976	− 150	160	$ 400
1976-77	Apr. 27, 1977	− 250	Jul. 25, 1977	− 170	80	$ 200
1977-78	Jun. 27, 1978	− 310	Dec. 30, 1977	− 210	100	$ 250
1978-79	Dec. 1, 1978	− 260	Apr. 10, 1979	+ 90	350	$ 875
1979-80	Mar. 26, 1980	− 600	Apr. 11, 1979	+ 55	655	$1,637
1980-81	May 12, 1981	− 685	Feb. 26, 1980	− 180	505	$1,262
1981-82	May 12, 1981	− 585	Jul. 27, 1982	− 300	285	$ 712
1982-83	Feb. 18, 1982	− 450	Nov. 4, 1982	− 220	230	$ 575
1983-84	Oct. 12, 1983	− 365	Jul. 23, 1984	− 230	135	$ 337
1984-85	Jun. 1, 1984	− 360	Jan. 22, 1985*	− 50	310	$ 775

* Through February 8, 1985—most recent data available

COPPER

L July - S December

Year	Dec. 1 Initiate Spread at	July 1 Liquidate Spread at	Maximum Adversity	Maximum Profitability	Gain/Loss	Spread Value
1972-73	− 150	+ 600	− $ 175	+ $1,875	+ 750	+ $1,875
1973-74	+ 370	+ 130	− $ 600	+ $1,575	− 240	− $ 600
1974-75	− 310	− 230	0	+ $ 275	+ 80	+ $ 200
1975-76	− 190	− 290	− $ 300	+ $ 100	− 100	− $ 250
1976-77	− 190	− 200	− $ 150	+ $ 25	− 10	− $ 25
1977-78	− 220	− 280	− $ 225	+ $ 25	− 60	− $ 150
1978-79	− 260	− 60	0	+ $ 875	+ 200	+ $ 500
1979-80	0	− 320	− $1,500	+ $ 25	− 320	− $ 800
1980-81	− 435	− 595	− $ 625	+ $ 100	− 160	− $ 400
1981-82	− 410	− 425	− $ 175	+ $ 63	− 15	− $ 37
1982-83	− 235	− 330	− $ 312	+ $ 37	− 95	− $ 237
1983-84	− 340	− 310	− $ 25	+ $ 75	+ 30	+ $ 75
1984-85	− 235	− 140	0	+ $ 463	+ 95	+ $1,237*

38% Correct in 13 Years

155 Points Net Profit

$387 Net profit

* Day-out February 8, 1985—latest data available

Figure 30
COPPER
(L Jul 84 - S Dec 84)

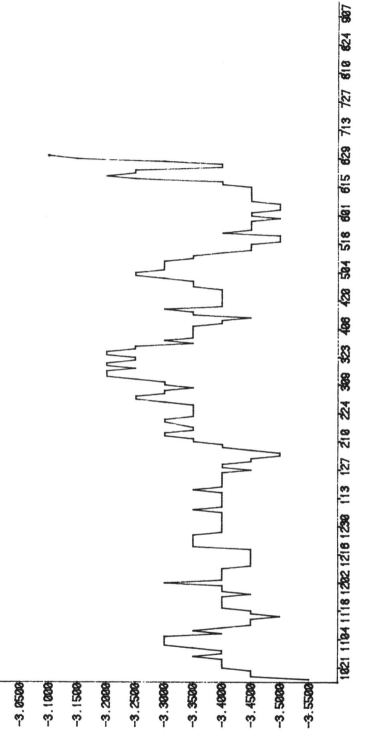

Figure 31
COPPER
(L Jul 83 - S Dec 83)

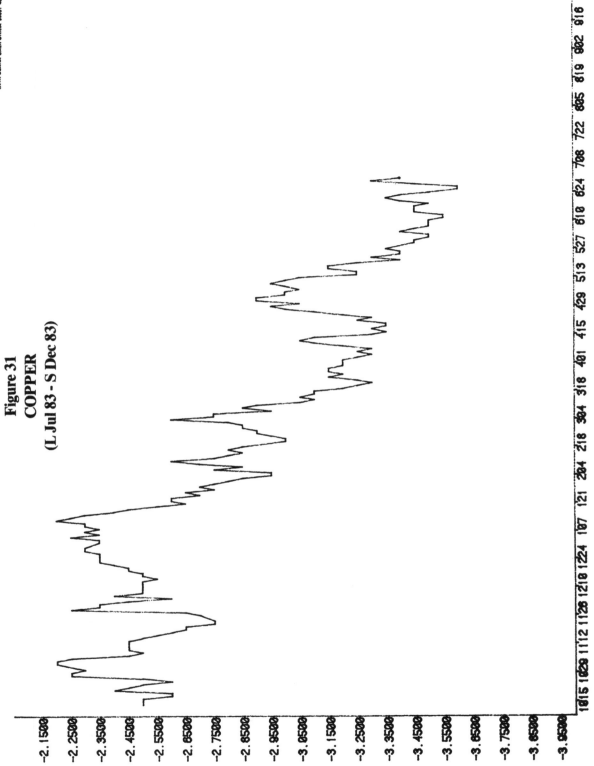

Part VI
Interdelivery Financial
Instrument Spreads

Chapter 19

Interest Rates

Most interest rate spreads are based on a very simple premise known as "yield curve analysis." Essentially, yield curve analysis attempts to determine how respective short- and longer-term interest rates will rise or fall over time, and how the change will be reflected in the market price of interest rate futures of different maturities. Since short-term rates are apt to be more volatile than long-term rates, the spread trader must determine the relationship that may develop over time of very near-term yields to longer-term yields. As a rule, when short-term interest rates rise very rapidly in the money market, there is a tendency for very near-term maturities to rise rapidly in yields versus longer maturities. The spread trader uses this information to know which months to buy and sell in designing his spread strategy.

Yield curves come in differing shapes, and change over time to reflect changing market conditions. Thus, a yield curve can be said to be positive or negative—or even flat. But the key to a successful analysis of a curve is its ultimate shape—whether it changes from, say, positive to negative or vice versa.

There are some standard rules that apply to placing interest rate spreads when the direction of the yield curve is known. They are:

1. When a yield curve is expected to change from positive to negative, a long deferred month versus a short nearby month spread should be placed.

2. When a yield curve is expected to change from negative to positive, a long nearby month versus a short deferred month spread should be placed.

Interest Rates

The difficulty, of course, comes from trying to correctly anticipate the direction of the yield curve. It is important to understand that yield is the inverse of price; thus, the higher the yield on an interest-bearing instrument, the lower the price—and vice versa. In other words, when yields rise, prices fall; and when yields decline, prices rise. Once understood, this inverse relationship makes a lot of sense. Traders who anticipate a boost in interest rates sell short interest rate futures; and traders who anticipate a decline in interest rates purchase interest rate futures (See Table 23 and results, together with Figures 32 and 33).

TRADING RULE

Buy March T-bill futures and sell December T-bill futures on October 15. Liquidate the spread on March 1. Please note that both contracts are for the same calendar year.

Table 23
TREASURY-BILLS
L March - S December

	Most negative difference			Most positive difference		
Year	Date	Spread Price Difference	Date	Spread Price Difference	Gain From Low to High	Spread Value
1976	Jan. 8, 1976	+ 51	Mar. 15, 1976	+234	183	$4,575
1976-77	Oct. 12, 1976	+ 57	Mar. 7, 1977	+212	155	$3,875
1977-78	Oct. 24, 1977	+ 54	Mar. 22, 1978	+129	75	$1,875
1978-79	Nov. 8, 1978	− 31	Aug. 15, 1978	+ 86	117	$2,925
1979-80	Mar. 10, 1980	−266	May 30, 1979	+ 18	284	$7,100
1980-81	Dec. 11, 1980	−299	May 16, 1980	+ 86	385	$9,625
1981-82	Aug. 25, 1981	− 91	Nov. 27, 1981	+100	191	$4,775
1982-83	Feb. 17, 1982	− 28	Dec. 3, 1982	+151	179	$4,475
1983-84	Jun. 20, 1983	+ 38	Mar. 14, 1984	+104	66	$1,650

TREASURY-BILLS
L March - S December

Year	Oct. 15 Initiate Spread at	Mar. 1 Liquidate Spread at	Maximum Adversity	Maximum Profitability	Gain/Loss	Spread Value
1976	+ 67	+206	−$ 400	+$3,475	+139	+$3,475
1976-77	+ 69	+204	−$ 50	+$3,375	+135	+$3,375
1977-78	+ 56	+107	−$ 50	+$1,350	+ 51	+$1,275
1978-79	+ 32	+ 22	−$1,575	+$ 50	− 10	−$ 250
1979-80	−193	−184	−$ 725	+$2,500	+ 9	+$ 225
1980-81	+ 3	−192	−$7,550	0	−195	−$4,875
1981-82	− 17	+ 41	−$1,525	+$2,925	+ 58	+$1,450
1982-83	+100	+ 36	−$1,600	+$1,275	− 64	−$1,600
1983-84	+ 64	+101	0	+$ 975	+ 37	+$ 925
1984-85	+ 86	+135	−$ 25	+$1,475	+ 49	+$1,225*

70% Correct in 10 Years

208 Points Net profit

$5,200 Net Profit

*Day out calculated as of February 8, 1985—latest data available

Figure 32
TREASURY-BILLS
(L Mar 84 - S Dec 84)

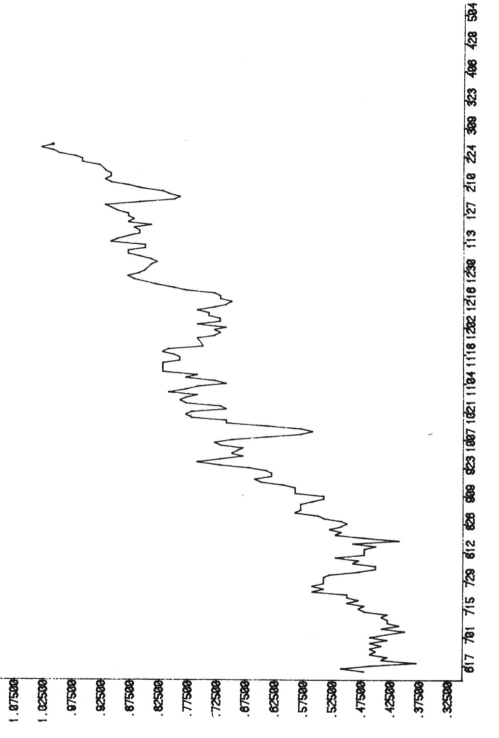

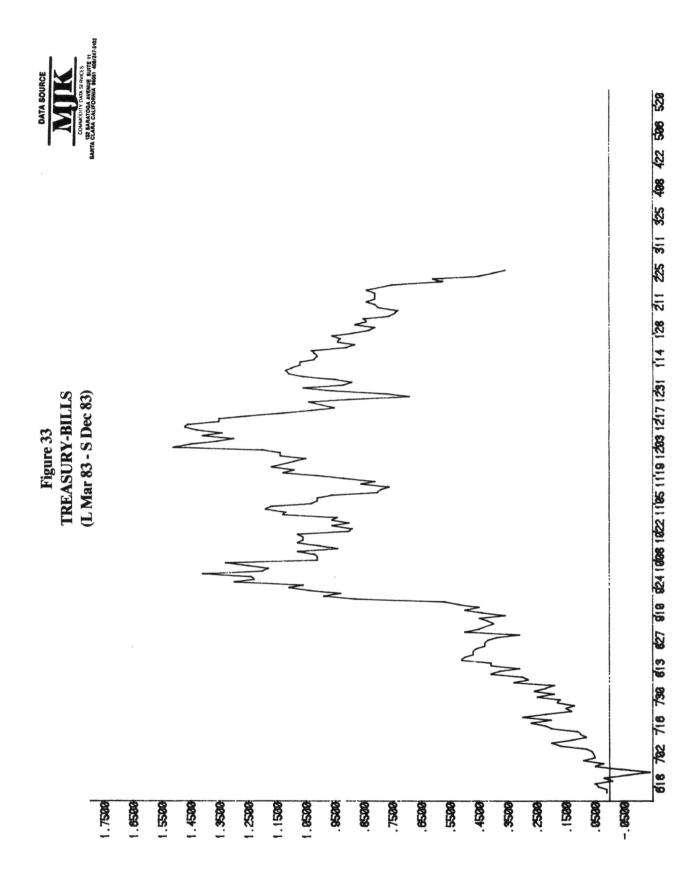

Figure 33
TREASURY-BILLS
(L Mar 83 - S Dec 83)

Part VII
Intermarket Spreads

Chapter 20

Chicago/
Kansas City Wheat

This intermarket spread, noted for its volatility, enjoys widespread popularity among spread traders—and deservedly so. The spread is quick to narrow or widen in response to the cross-currents of buying and selling sweeping the two markets, and it has a fairly reliable seasonality. Before you consider the Chicago-Kansas City intermarket wheat spread, however, there are a few things you should know. First, it is unlikely you will receive lower spread commissions and margins in trading this spread. So be prepared to deposit more funds with your broker than you normally would to spread, say, two months on the Board of Trade. Second, always remember that the Chicago contract will typically be stronger or weaker than Kansas City, depending on the direction of the market. Thus, in a bull market, Chicago will rise faster; in a bear market, Chicago will decline faster. However, when the market becomes so overwhelmingly one-sided that a string of limit moves might occur, Kansas City may temporarily provide the price leadership for one simple reason—the daily limit of the Kansas City is larger, 25 cents compared with just 20 cents for Chicago wheat.

Traditionally, the transportation costs between Chicago and Kansas City were a key ingredient of the spread price. Theoretically, if not in practice, a spread trader could buy the lower priced wheat and take delivery. He would then ship the wheat north to Chicago or south to Kansas City—whichever market he was short—and deliver against his short. The difference in price above transportation costs would constitute his profit. Actually, this rarely happens, because the two wheat contracts are different. Chicago trades Soft Red winter wheat and Kansas City trades Hard Red winter wheat. The two different wheats have different uses and are difficult to substitute for one another. The Kansas City Hard Red winter wheat is used primarily for export, whereas the wheat traded in Chicago is used domestically. Nevertheless, the two markets are aggressively spread by speculators and trade interests. In fact, to pick up a quick profit in this spread, a spread trader might carefully monitor the spreading activities of the commercial interests and then follow their direction. The spreading activities of the trade frequently provide the key to the future direction of the spread.

CHICAGO JULY WHEAT VS. KANSAS CITY JULY WHEAT

Although this spread offers a number of opportunities throughout the year, the most consistent appears to be the long Chicago-short Kansas City wheat spread placed at the beginning of March and held until mid-June. The nice thing about this spread is that even in the years that it doesn't work, the loss is minimal—usually you can get out at about breakeven. And, in a good year, such as 1979, you can pick up at least 15 cents. Because you are spreading two different markets, in this instance it helps to give the floor broker some freedom in putting it on and unwinding the spread. A discretion of, say, two cents and a skillful broker can often spell the difference between a profit and loss on this spread (See Table 24 and results, together with Figures 34 and 35).

TRADING RULE

Buy Chicago July wheat and sell Kansas City July wheat on March 1. Liquidate the spread on June 20.

Table 24
CHICAGO VS. KANSAS CITY WHEAT
L Chicago July Wheat - S Kansas City July Wheat

	Most negative difference		Most positive difference			
Year	**Date**	**Spread Price Difference**	**Date**	**Spread Price Difference**	**Gain From Low to High**	**Spread Value**
1976	May 5, 1976	−16¢	July 2, 1976	− 4¢	12¢	$ 600
1976-77	Aug. 2, 1976	− 8½¢	Feb. 18, 1977	+10½¢	19¢	$ 950
1977-78	Dec. 5, 1977	− 2½¢	May 30, 1978	+20¼¢	22¾¢	$1,137
1978-79	Jul. 26, 1978	−11¢	Jun. 22, 1979	+27¾¢	38¾¢	$1,937
1979-80	Apr. 18, 1980	− 9¼¢	Oct. 3, 1979	+22½¢	31¾¢	$1,587
1980-81	Jun. 29, 1981	−37¾¢	Jul. 31, 1980	+20¼¢	58¢	$2,900
1981-82	Jul. 19, 1982	−37¾¢	Oct. 12, 1981	+10½¢	48¼¢	$2,412
1982-83	Mar. 8, 1983	−34¾¢	Aug. 13, 1982	+ 1½¢	36¼¢	$1,812
1983-84	Jul. 16, 1984	−20¾¢	Aug. 31, 1983	+11½¢	32¼¢	$1,612
1984-85	Jul. 25, 1984	−16½¢	Feb. 7, 1985*	+ ¼¢	16¾¢	$ 837

* Through February 8, 1985—most recent data available

CHICAGO/KANSAS CITY WHEAT
L Chicago July Wheat - S Kansas City July Wheat

Year	**Mar. 1 Initiate Spread at**	**Jun. 20 Liquidate Spread at**	**Maximum Adversity**	**Maximum Profitability**	**Gain/Loss**	**Spread Value**
1976	−14¢	− 7½¢	−$ 100	+ 413	+ 6½¢	+$ 325
1977	Data Not Available for 1977					
1978	+ 4¢	+13¾¢	−$ 25	+$ 813	+ 9¾¢	+$ 488
1979	+10¾¢	+22¾¢	−$ 175	+$ 600	+12¢	+$ 600
1980	+ 2¾¢	+ 2¾¢	−$ 600	+$ 150	0	0
1981	− 5¼¢	−26½¢	−$1,063	0	−21¼¢	−$1,063
1982	−14½¢	−21¾¢	−$ 600	+$ 88	− 7¼¢	−$ 363
1983	−33¼¢	− 9¼¢	−$ 75	+$1,400	+24¢	+$1,200
1984	−16¾¢	−11½¢	−$ 100	+$ 625	+ 5¼¢	+$ 263

62% Correct in 8 Years

29¢ Net profit

$1,450 Net profit

Figure 34
CHICAGO/KANSAS CITY WHEAT
(L Jul 84 Chi Wheat - S Jul 84 KC Wheat)

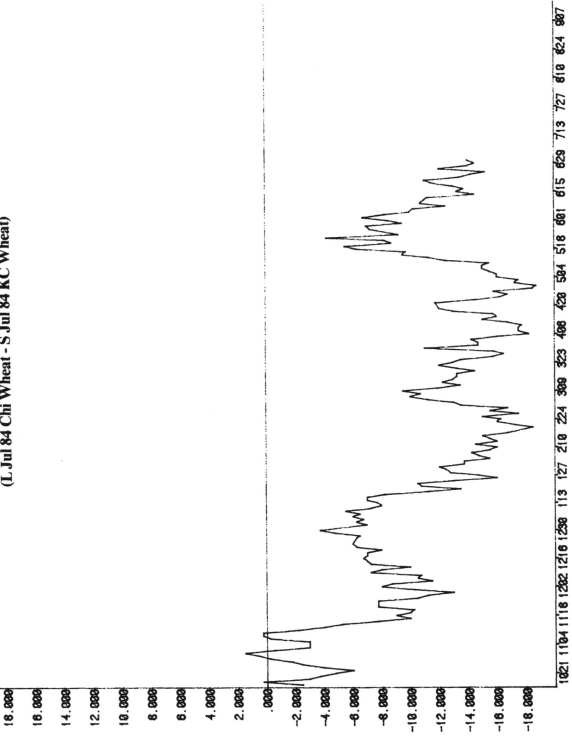

162

Figure 35
CHICAGO/KANSAS CITY WHEAT
(L Jul 83 Chi Wheat - S Jul 83 KC Wheat)

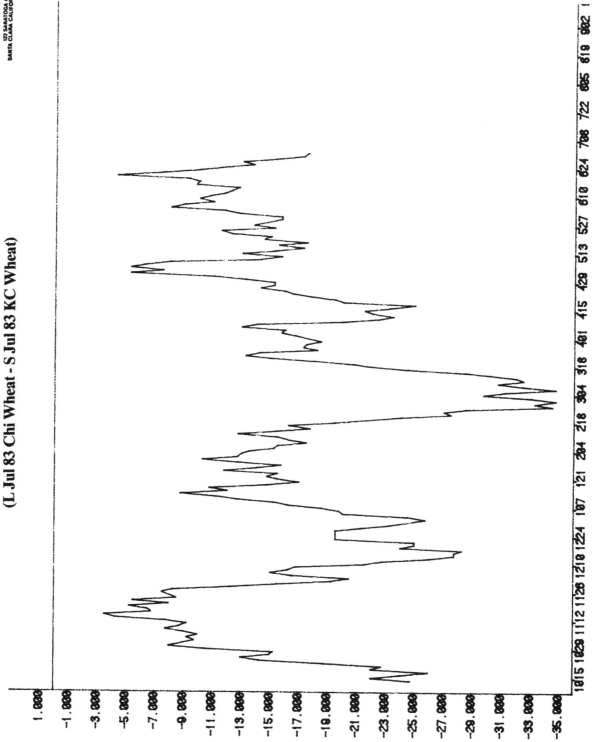

163

CPSIA information can be obtained
at www.ICGtesting.com
Printed in the USA
LVHW102037061218
599550LV00007B/14/P